William Arthur

'A very dear friend of mine; one who, for his eloquence, his nobility of character, and his general ability, was the first man in our Church – the Rev. William Arthur' (Dr J.H. Rigg to Dr Benson, the Archbishop of Canterbury, 19 October 1895).

William Arthur

First among Methodists

Norman W. Taggart

EPWORTH PRESS

In memory of my parents, Katie and Bill

The original painting of the cover portrait of William
Arthur is owned by Mr Peter Arthur of Edinburgh, who
is the great-great-grandson of William Arthur's younger
brother, Alexander. The author and publishers are
grateful to him for permitting it to be used in this
biography.
The photographer is Mr Ken Paterson, Laundry Flat,
Newliston House, Kirkliston, West Lothian, EH29 9EB.
The publishers also wish to express their appreciation
of the assistance they have received from Mr R.H.
Hunting, a distant relative of William Arthur.

07162 0489 4

First published 1993
by Epworth Press
1 Central Buildings, Westminster, London SW1H 9NR

Phototypeset by Intype, London
Printed in Great Britain by
Mackays of Chatham, Kent

Contents

Preface

William Arthur – Wesleyan Methodist preacher, writer and statesman – was a leading Christian in the second half of the nineteenth century. His years, 1819 to 1901, coincided with those of Queen Victoria. T.B. Stephenson in his useful *William Arthur, a Brief Biography* (1907), admitted the limitations of his study, and expressed the hope that a fuller account of Arthur's life and work would appear. It is remarkable that this task was not undertaken earlier.

Arthur once claimed that biographers resembled portrait painters in that they tended to present idealized pictures of their subjects. In the preface to his biography of Samuel Budgett, a Wesleyan Methodist businessman, Arthur wrote that he would insert 'every real scar'[1] I can do no better than seek to follow Arthur's lead in this. History rather than hagiography is my aim.

It is a considerable honour and responsibility to write this book. Arthur and I have much in common. We were both born in the northern part of Ireland, and have lived in the west of Ireland. We have both served in India, for much shorter periods than either of us would have wished for reasons beyond our control. We have both worked at the London headquarters of Methodist overseas missions. I am conscious, however, that Arthur's intellectual, literary and spiritual gifts far exceeded mine. I can only hope that despite my limitations Arthur's greatness will shine through these pages.

The book seeks to help the reader who is interested in history to discover Arthur as a significant Wesleyan Methodist figure. Arthur's interests were diverse, and included mission, education, philosophy, politics, pan-evangelicalism and Roman Catholicism. His views were often expressed in forthright and controversial terms, and provide fascinating insights into public debates then and now.

I returned to serious study and writing in my forties, in the midst of an already busy life. Apart from 1977 to 1979, when at the end of a period in London with the Methodist Church Overseas Division I was given study-leave by the Methodist Church in Ireland, research and writing have been part-time activities for me. Occasional spare hours, less busy periods of the year, and annual holiday leave, have all been used as much as possible for reading and writing. Each of the three main projects I have completed – a Ph.D. degree, my first book and now this book – has taken approximately five years. This has required an enormous amount of good will and support from my wife, Margaret, and much tolerance at times from other members of the family. From myself it has called for considerable discipline and persistence, with a high level of motivation. It has, however, been worthwhile. My life has been greatly enriched, and my ministry has benefitted in many ways.

I have received support from longstanding and newly-acquired friends. Professional scholars nowadays frequently work under extremely trying circumstances, yet I have received nothing but courtesy and kindness from them. Epworth Press, my publishers, have also been unfailingly helpful, even when pressing me hard, as they must, on practical matters.

Cyril Davey, Dr D.W. Bebbington, Dr D. Hempton, Shelagh Livingstone, J. Munsey Turner, Dr John Vickers, and my wife, have all read complete drafts. Their suggestions, often from specialist view-points, have been extremely valuable. Others have advised and commented on specific parts, or allowed me to see unpublished or rare material. These include Professor John M. Barkley, Dr R.J. Carwardine, Professor J.A. Faris, Dr Brian Fitzpatrick, John A. Gamble, Dr Ambrose Macaulay, Tim S.A. Maquiban, Professor J. Stanley McQuade, Professor Kenneth E. Rowe, Dr R. Alan Russell, Professor W.P. Stephens and Dr Frank Wright. All comments have been appreciated and taken seriously. Many have been incorporated in the text, but I alone bear responsibility for remaining flaws.

The final stages of preparation for publication have had to be completed in Colombo, far from the libraries and archival collections where much of the research took place, far too from some of my own resource material. This accounts for minor discrepancies in presentation of the Notes and Bibliography.

A grant from the Methodist Church Overseas Division went some way towards meeting research costs. An anonymous gift, and other forms of help, greatly facilitated publication.

Lower Ballinderry, Northern Ireland   Norman Taggart
Colombo, Sri Lanka   December 1992

1

William Arthur, 1819–1901

William Arthur has been described as a man of broad and statesmanlike views on public questions, one who was fearless in opposition to oppression. His spirituality, skill with the spoken and written word in several languages, grasp of missionary problems and opportunities, concern for the well-being of the church, and intellectual vigour, have all drawn favourable comment. Two writers in our own day have referred to him as 'brilliant and saintly'[1] and an 'astute Wesleyan theologian'.[2] A contemporary, writing to the Archbishop of Canterbury, simply described him as Methodism's 'first man'.[3]

Early Years in Ireland (1819–1837)

Arthur was born on 3 February 1819, and lived in Kells, Co. Antrim, in the north-eastern part of Ireland. His mother, Margaret (née Kennedy), was descended from a Scottish family of which one member, because of Jacobite sympathies, found it prudent to flee across the Irish Sea to settle in Ulster around the time of the 1715 Rebellion. He prospered in Ireland, and it was his grandson who became William Arthur's maternal grandfather. William's father, James, was said to be descended from prominent families in Counties Clare and Limerick. The Arthurs belonged to the Church of Ireland (Episcopalian).

Kells and the surrounding countryside have early Christian connections.[4] The village itself was formerly the seat of an abbey, and the adjoining village of Connor has given its name to a bishopric. Not many miles away stands Slemish, a mountain associated with Patrick, patron saint of Ireland, in the days of his captivity.

Because of now-unknown 'family misfortunes'[5] the Arthurs

were forced to uproot themselves from Kells when William was twelve. They settled at Newport in Co. Mayo in the west of Ireland. This is an area steeped in history and of outstanding natural beauty. A prominent feature is Croagh Patrick, another mountain associated with Patrick, on which he is said to have prayed for forty days in AD 441. John Wesley climbed to the top on a hot day in May 1762, but was unimpressed. He preached in Newport later on the same day, and in nearby Westport the next morning. W.M. Thackeray visited the area in 1842, a decade after the Arthurs made their home in Newport, and was entranced by the scenery.

The beautiful and historic countryside in which Arthur grew up would have made a deep and lasting impression on a young mind that was claimed to be of 'a poetic cast'.[6] It has been said that as a boy he was 'steeped . . . in poetry', and that he knew many of Byron's poems by heart.[7] His acute powers of observation enabled him to store up mental pictures of his homeland that stayed with him throughout his life and were often his points of reference and comparison.

We can only speculate about Arthur's education. It was probably partly informal and in part under a tutor. There is a report that for a time he received instruction from a man who had been trained for the Roman Catholic priesthood but who refused to take holy orders.[8] Another source suggests that he attended a school run by a Presbyterian minister.[9] He also appears to have attended an Episcopal Sunday School in Newport where his promise and progress were noted by the local Church of Ireland rector.

In his early teens Arthur entered the business of his father's friend, George Woods, described in some sources as a corn merchant in Westport.[10] It soon became evident, however, that Arthur was more interested in the bread of life than the bread which perishes. It is of interest that the window which commemorates him in Wesley's Chapel, London, is entitled 'The Sower'.

In 1834 the Wesleyan Methodist Conference in Ireland appointed John Holmes as Superintendent of the Castlebar Circuit. He remained until 1837, and had a particularly fruitful ministry, especially in Westport. People from other churches associated with the local Methodists in their services, and received great blessing. When the Church of Ireland rector in Newport was told of these developments he is reported to have expressed confidence that William Arthur was 'too wise a bird to be caught with Methodist chaff'.[11] Events proved him wrong, however, and within a short time Arthur joined the Methodists. It is reported that the service at which he was converted in Westport was attended by only three people including the preacher, John Holmes. The formal Wesleyan Methodist membership probably remained comparatively small. Although Thackeray referred to Anglicans, Presbyterians and Roman Catholics when visiting Westport in 1842, he made no mention of Methodists.

When not quite sixteen years of age, Arthur made his first attempts at preaching. Despite initial parental opposition, he progressed rapidly and completed the preliminary steps required prior to entering the Wesleyan Methodist ministry. He was accepted as a ministerial candidate in 1837, having already demonstrated his gifts for some months on the Sligo Circuit. His strong faith, resistance to assumptions of Anglican superiority, and opposition to Roman Catholicism, particularly as manifested by its priests, were abiding features of Arthur's life. These characteristics were probably the result of those few years spent as a convert to Methodism in the west of Ireland. Home and family influences on Arthur are again discussed later.[12]

A story is told of Arthur's designation for overseas service under the Wesleyan Methodist Missionary Society (WMMS). Jabez Bunting presided over the Wesleyan Methodist Conference in Ireland at which Arthur was received as a candidate for the ministry. He was impressed by what he saw and heard of him, and is reported to have remarked that he would like him for overseas missions. Thomas Waugh, a senior Irish Wesleyan preacher, is said to have replied, 'We will not give him to you, but we will lend him to you.'[13] Years later the loan was reclaimed when Arthur was put in charge of the new Methodist College in Belfast.

Understandably, Newport and Westport held a special place in Arthur's affections. His mother became postmistress in Newport.[14] There is evidence to suggest that his father died there in 1844 or 1845, a time of famine.[15] Conditions were severe throughout the west of Ireland, with Westport reported to be in an 'indescribable' state, 'a nest of fever and vermin'.[16] This may have been a factor in James Arthur's death. William's mother emigrated to America around the same period, possibly also because of the famine. She died there in 1855.[17] In 1852 Arthur, by then resident in London, supported a move to have Newport and Westport designated by the Wesleyans as an area for mission. A Wesleyan Methodist chapel was built in Newport in 1857, close to where the Arthur family had lived. It was sold to the Roman Catholics in 1909, and was replaced in 1940 by a community hall. Arthur contributed to the building of a new Wesleyan Methodist chapel in Westport in 1875, on the site of the one in which he had been converted. The building still stands on the Mall, but is now used as a store. There is no active Methodist witness in the region today.

From Mayo to Mysore (1837–1841)

In 1837, Arthur was sent to the Theological Institution at Hoxton, London, Wesleyan Methodism's first college for ministerial training. It had already been used by others for many years as a training centre. Robert Morrison of China studied there from 1803 to 1807, and the London Missionary Society made use of it from 1826 to 1830. When the Wesleyan Methodists took over the premises, Dr Jabez Bunting was appointed President, and Dr John Hanna Theological Tutor.

Classes had commenced in 1834. In Arthur's first year, John Hunt and James Calvert, who both served later in Fiji, were fellow-students. It was a time of spiritual awakening and renewal, with students sharing in class-meetings and pouring out their hearts to God in prayer. Arthur's awareness of, and thinking about, the Holy Spirit is said to have been greatly stimulated in this period, and remained an abiding interest throughout his life. His effectiveness as a preacher was noted, when it was claimed that he never preached without seeing conversions.[18] His ministry was to diversify over the years, but he always retained his evangelical zeal. His interest in India, to which he was appointed by the WMMS, was also aroused and greatly stimulated at this time.

For two years Arthur seized the opportunity to learn, reading avidly and benefitting much from his contacts with staff and students. The neighbourhood around Hoxton was described as not 'the choicest', and its rooms 'small and gloomy'[19] and too few to accommodate all the students. Arthur was therefore housed with Elijah Hoole, a Secretary of the WMMS who had spent eight years in India. On his return from India Hoole had superintended WMMS schools in Ireland, so he and Arthur would have had much to discuss.

During his years at Hoxton Arthur displayed great aptitude for learning, and laid the foundation for a life of disciplined study and service. He gave early evidence of what became permanent features of his ministry, for example his concern for basic principles, thoroughness and integrity. As an 'out-door' student, not resident in the Institution, he was required to be at Hoxton by half-past six in the morning in winter, and half an hour earlier in summer.

On the Sunday afternoon of 14 April 1839, Arthur and three other missionaries – John Garrett, George Pope and E.G. Squarebridge – were commended to the care of God at a special service held in Wesley's Chapel, London. Next morning they embarked at Gravesend on board the *Essex* bound for Madras. Two of the WMMS Secretaries, Drs Hoole and Bunting, accompanied them on board and again sought God's blessing on their enterprise. The vessel was a fine new ship of nearly eight hundred tons, well staffed and equipped. The new missionaries were tokens of an increased commitment to India by Wesleyan Methodism. All the signs were good. There was certainly nothing to suggest that in two years Squarebridge would have died of cholera, and Arthur would have returned to England in poor health.

On the voyage to India, a distant view of Madeira reminded Arthur of Clare Island as it stretched across the mouth of 'the incomparable Clew Bay' in Co. Mayo, sheltering the armaments of the pirate Queen, Grace O'Malley, from her Elizabethan foes.[20] The voyage took them round the Cape of Good Hope. The journey went well by the standards of the day, despite storms and deaths. Arthur had a fall on deck and suffered from regular bouts of seasickness until the ship entered the less troubled seas of the tropics. Despite cramped conditions, with no desk or table and with the violent pitching of the vessel, he made progress with the Kanarese

language, a study already begun in England. Great was his sense
of expectation when, after eighteen weeks at sea, he was able at
last to pick out the Indian coast. As they neared Madras itself he
observed St Thomas's Mount, the traditional site of the apostle's
martyrdom, the spire of St Andrew's Church and Fort St George.

Missionary colleagues received Arthur and his travelling com-
panions on Indian soil. Three of the new arrivals, including
Arthur, were to proceed to Mysore, with one remaining in
Madras. But for almost a month they remained together in
Madras, visiting places of interest and meeting people. Historical
sites, climate, customs, transport, religious practice and people
were all described by Arthur in detail. Climbing St Thomas's
Mount, he commented that it was to Roman Catholics in India
what Croagh Patrick was to their co-religionists in Ireland.[21]
Those to whom he spoke were of the opinion that Roman Catholic
converts differed little from their non-Christian neighbours in
culture, morality, or religious practice. On one occasion he met
with the missionaries of the Protestant churches working in the
city. Episcopalians, Presbyterians, Independents and Wesleyans
all gathered together, reflecting a refreshing though still modest
degree of fellowship and co-operation.[22] An English-language
school run by the Church of Scotland was noted by Arthur. This
later became the prestigious Madras Christian College. Taking
everything into account, and without denying that the total
Christian resources were slender, Arthur held the view that faith
and morale were high among Christians in a city 'given to
idolatry'. Multitudes there were without Christ and therefore
were 'hopeless and unholy', he reflected.[23]

At sunset on 27 August 1839 Arthur and the other Mysore
missionaries set out for Bangalore. The journey, which he recorded
in vivid detail, took them through Arcot, Vellore and Kolar. Their
main means of transport were palanquins. Though these had no
wheels, Arthur described them as 'dwarf omnibuses'.[24] Each
vehicle had a team of twelve bearers of whom six carried at a time
for periods of seven or eight minutes, the spare bearers running
alongside. It was a form of transport of which Arthur disapproved
because it used people as beasts of burden. Coolies were also
employed to carry the baggage, keeping pace with the palanquins
with boxes suspended from long bamboos laid across their

shoulders. Arthur welcomed the opportunity to ride by pony for part of the way. They avoided the hottest time of the day, and travelled by night with the help of torches. Arthur continued to give detailed accounts of much that he saw, including a local blacksmith at work, irrigation methods in a country where water is always precious, and the splendid mountain scenery through which they passed as they climbed in the Eastern Ghats. Once they stopped at a place where a London Missionary Society worker was based. He, claimed Arthur, was the only Christian missionary in the two hundred miles between Madras and Bangalore. The spiritual plight of the people and their neglect by Christians in other parts of the world made a deep impression on him.

On 6 September they reached Bangalore, where Hoole and a colleague had started the Wesleyan mission in 1821. Arthur was immediately struck by the British military presence and by the orderliness of the cantonment area, where troops were quartered and Europeans lived. In the city itself he observed with his usual perception various people at work: the banker seated on the floor with his scales to weigh coins and a stone to test gold; also the draper, grocer and coppersmith. He had praise for the London Missionary Society, the first Protestant mission to work in the Kanarese language, but he was sharply critical of Roman Catholic work. In particular, he attacked their practice of presenting biblical material in the form of drama, dismissing such efforts as 'barbarous theatricals' which trivialized the essential Christian message.[25] Later generations of Methodists would encourage initiatives of this kind, aware of the need for variety in communication. The Wesleyan work in the city was divided according to language, English, Tamil and Kanarese. There was much to encourage on all three fronts, claimed Arthur. Some Europeans had been led to faith in Jesus Christ, and Tamil enquirers came to the mission house for baptismal instruction. The Kanarese work interested Arthur most. He noted carefully the saving themes in the street preaching of missionary colleagues:

> The unity of God, His spirituality and holiness, the corrupt heart and guilty life of man, the certainty that these will entail punishment, the incompetence of penance or idols to save,

and the wonderful atonement of Christ, whereby pardon is made just and renewal of heart possible.[26]

On the basis of such truths, and since it appeared that Roman Catholics locally were as much committed to an idolatrous system as the Hindus, Arthur and his missionary colleagues did not doubt that it was necessary for them to make clear that Protestantism and Roman Catholicism differed so much as to be separate religions.[27] Arthur welcomed the fact that the Wesleyan work in Kanarese in Bangalore involved a Sunday School, six day schools and a school for orphan girls. Here Indian children could receive sound Christian teaching rather than the 'filthy mythology' of Hinduism.[28] In contrast to the traditional prejudice against the education of girls, Arthur stressed the peculiar importance of this side of the work. 'Every man born in . . . India', he claimed, 'has been doomed to be the son of a mother studiously consigned to unmitigated ignorance.'[29]

Gubbi was Arthur's final destination. It had been chosen as the headquarters of the Wesleyan mission in the Kanarese-speaking area after a seven-week tour in 1836 by Thomas Hodson, who had been transferred from Calcutta to Bangalore. He had been asked by the Wesleyan Missionary Committee to go to Mysore and the surrounding area, with a view to extending their work. His report highlighted the claims of Gubbi, a town with a population of about five thousand. Set in fertile country within reach of several large villages, it was, reported Hodson, about fifty miles north-west of Bangalore and twelve miles west of Tumkur:

> There is not a large temple in the whole district. There is very little Brahminical influence, there are no English bad examples, no Roman Catholics, no mixed population. The . . . Collector, or Superintendent, will aid us . . .; it is the centre of the Mysore country; we shall have nobody to interfere with us.[30]

Gubbi was in fact an important centre for Lingayats, the followers of a twelfth-century movement, Vira-Shaivism, within Hinduism which rejected the caste system, temple worship and the high status of Brahmans.

Hodson's report indicated a bold new strategy. He had outlined it in general terms at the end of his period in Calcutta, an approach which could be described as an 'intensive' rather than the traditional 'scatter' method. Missionaries, he argued, needed to concentrate on the heathen, not Europeans. They should not be stationed too far apart, but should be strategically placed so that they could consult and work together. Mission house, school and church should be more closely integrated. There should be one specialist school to which more promising pupils could be sent, with a view to raising a native ministry.

Hodson first visited Gubbi in August 1836, and settled there some months later with his wife. In 1838 he proceeded to Mysore city, and was replaced in Gubbi by John Jenkins. Arthur's appointment was to work with Jenkins, to strengthen the mission.

As Arthur recorded, it was a cloudless day on 9 October when he set off from Bangalore for Gubbi with Jenkins. As they passed through a chain of hills, Arthur made special reference to Shivaganga as 'a high conical peak, not less sacred here' than Croagh Patrick in the west of Ireland.[31] Remembering a holy well in Co. Mayo, in which there was thought to be a holy trout, he acknowledged that idolatry with all its emptiness and absurdity was not confined to India and to Hinduism. After a night at Tumkur they started out again. Eventually, on 11 October, Arthur stood before the small white mission house at Gubbi:

> Never did I approach a spot with such feelings. It was a lonely home, but it was a post of glorious duty. There was no Christian congregation with whom to worship, but there was the God whom Christians adore. The people never hailed a Sabbath, nor observed a sacrament, but in another generation they should . . . It was sweet, after six months of wayfaring, to bow before God on the very spot to which all your journeys had been directed.[32]

Arthur's assessment of the situation was accurate. Records of the period confirm that the only church members were the families of missionaries, the only baptisms being those of missionaries' children. It was, by Arthur's account, an extremely isolated circuit, some forty miles long and fifteen wide. The next mission station to the east was Bangalore, sixty miles away. To the south was Mysore city, ninety miles distant; to the north, Bellary, two hundred miles; and to the west, Mangalore, also two hundred miles. But people were civil and courteous, ready to listen to the missionaries with respect. Twenty villages and towns close to Gubbi were as open to the Christian missionary as to the Brahman priest. 'There never was before the Church such a field', Arthur declared. To leave it untilled for lack of resources, either human or material, would be an instance of 'shortsighted and scandalous neglect.'[33]

As he contemplated his field of service, Arthur felt deeply for the deprived, especially the outcastes, women and child-widows. He wrote of the multiplicity of Hindu gods, paying particular attention to those of special importance in and around Gubbi. He ridiculed the endless variety of Hindu objects of worship, animate and inanimate, reserving his most stringent criticism for the lingam, usually in the form of a black stone shaped like a penis, associated with the worship of Shiva. This he saw as a special affront to man's conscience and to God's dignity, an example of satan's audacious inspiration.[34]

Arthur took up the challenge of his appointment with enthusiasm, accompanying missionary colleagues in street preaching and meeting with them for urgent and sustained prayer on behalf of the work. There was normally a resident missionary colleague with him, and occasionally others visited the Gubbi circuit or he visited them. A gifted linguist, he applied himself to a disciplined study of the language, convinced that a high level of accomplishment was crucial for an effective presentation of the gospel. A language teacher had been engaged for him, with whom he worked daily, and by all accounts his progress was phenomenal. Indeed he was able to read a Bible passage in Kanarese at the first Sunday service he attended in Gubbi on 13 October.

The usual routine each Sunday was to hold a service in a schoolroom in the town at six o'clock in the morning, and others at half-past ten in the church, at four in the market, and in the evening an English service at the mission house. Other meetings were held elsewhere during the week, usually in the mornings. The temple entrance in Gubbi was a favourite place, the message uncompromising:

Within hearing of the altar, it was a stirring thing to stand and tell them all the truth, to tell them that their god was an idol, that their services were folly, that their worship was sin, and that there was 'one God, and one Mediator between God and man, the man Christ Jesus'.[35]

Arthur never actually entered a Hindu temple. To have done so, he would have been required to remove his shoes. That, he believed, would have compromised his position, implying acceptance in some sense of other gods.

The Friday evening meeting was generally of a conversational nature, perhaps in a shop or in some other public meeting place. If necessary, as an encouragement, the preachers would first engage the people in everyday conversation, and then steer the discussion towards religious topics. Controversy was normally entered into with good humour, though sometimes a Brahman would lose his temper and abuse them. This did little damage to the missionaries' case since, according to Arthur, their listeners were generally of the opinion that those who became angry in debate forfeited the argument.

Other places visited within the circuit included Bidare, Chelur, Kunigal and Tumkur. Schools were established in as many centres as possible, under teachers who worked to a set syllabus. Although many of the teachers and pupils were Hindus, the main thrust of the curriculum was openly Christian with the emphasis on reading, learning the scriptures (especially the Psalms, with their focus on the holiness of God and the evils of idolatry), and catechetical instruction. The missionaries monitored progress each month. In addition to preaching, the distribution of scripture portions and religious tracts took place regularly. Informal contacts were also recognized as important. Arthur's study door at Gubbi was often open. It led to a verandah where people gathered to talk to him. On free evenings he went for a stroll, engaging in conversation with whomever he happened to meet.

Arthur was wholly taken up in the work, and all seemed set for a period of growth. When Jenkins was appointed to Bangalore, he was succeeded in Gubbi by Matthew Male, to maintain the principle of having two missionaries on the station. Tragedy soon struck, however. Male's two little children were in poor health, and medical help was two days distant. They became ill and died within a short time of each other in 1840, and were buried beside the mission house in Gubbi.[36] Squarebridge too became ill at Kunigal, and died of cholera.[37] The sorrows of 1840 were not yet at an end. Failing eyesight and a general worsening of his health forced Arthur to seek medical advice in Bangalore and Madras. A change of climate in the Nilgiri Hills failed to restore him, and a decision was taken that he should return immediately to Britain. Arthur was devastated. The people had become 'inexpressibly dear' to him in the short period he had been with them. He wept more on leaving them than on parting from his home:

> My missionary race was short. God made it so. But, looking back ... I would not for the universe have that brief space blotted from my experience.[38]

On 20 April 1841, Arthur embarked at Madras in a leaky, ill-equipped ship to return to Britain. It was a horrendous journey. The crew was drunken, argumentative and incompetent. The provisions were meagre and of poor quality. To make matters worse, several deaths took place including those of the captain and his wife. Arthur, not a good sailor under the best of conditions, and despite being ill and in low spirits, had to help man the vessel and plot its course. Eventually, after encountering danger and privation, he and another passenger negotiated a passage on another ship and transferred to it while still on the high seas. Thankful to be alive, they reached Britain on 26 September.

Not surprisingly, progress at Gubbi remained slow following this series of set-backs. The first converts, a man of the washerman caste and his four sons, were not baptized until 1843. With the benefit of hindsight it can be seen that Tumkur would have made a better centre, being less remote and providing the headquarters of the Collector, an important government official. Indeed Gubbi was abandoned for a period in the 1850s, the mission house and chapel being sold. It was only after the appointment of a missionary to Tumkur that the work improved generally, partly due to the encouragement and help received from the Collector. A fresh start then became possible in Gubbi.

Gubbi is today a taluq (district) headquarters, housing the district court and some other official buildings. The work begun by Wesleyan missionaries is now part of the Church of South India, within the Karnataka Central Diocese. Gubbi is still recognized as the oldest centre of Methodist witness in the region, and in recent times the town's name has been given to a village and rural uplift programme, the Gubbi Mission. The present church building preserves the association with Arthur, being opened as a memorial to him in 1903, two years after his death.

From President's Assistant to President (1841–1867)

On his return to Britain Arthur was placed under medical attention for ten months, and accepted only occasional speaking engagements. Initially not allowed to read or write, he mentally prepared his addresses with great thoroughness and delivered them without notes. He was made available to the WMMS which at once recognized his outstanding ability in the advocacy of missions. Arthur's appearance – pale face, frail body and tinted spectacles to protect his eyes – added to the pathos and power of his appeals on behalf of India's millions, as for example at the anniversary meeting of the WMMS in May 1842:

> Nine European Missionary Ministers of our Body amongst five hundred millions of men! Was that the true representation of Wesleyan zeal and Wesleyan love? Did we expect that nine men were to take an adequate share in carrying out this moral revolution there? . . . Could the friends of Missions look at all those millions, and contemplate each of them in the aspect of a brother, and then say that they had done all they could and would do?[39]

In 1843, while continuing his association with the WMMS, Arthur was appointed to Wesley's Chapel, London, to assist John Scott, President of the Conference and the leading Wesleyan Methodist educationist at that time. This appointment was renewed in 1844. Arthur saw great potential and challenge in the work at Wesley's Chapel. Aware of revival in Hinde Street chapel, also in London, he wrote that there seemed to be 'no reason in God or Scripture' why a thousand members should not be added at Wesley's Chapel.[40] At the Conference of 1845, he was again made available to the WMMS, but questions were asked about the reasons for this special arrangement. Dr Bunting replied that as an Irishman Arthur could not be sent to an English circuit, and that, health permitting, Arthur hoped to return overseas. Some months later, however, Arthur wrote to his friend James H. Rigg that trouble with his eyes still restricted his reading.

Arthur's reputation soared in the mid–1840s. He was in constant demand throughout the Wesleyan connexion as a public speaker and preacher. His appearance at a missionary event or a chapel anniversary helped to draw a crowd and boosted the financial response. His availability coincided with the height of 'railway mania', and written invitations to him to preach were often accompanied by relevant information about convenient trains.

In 1846 Arthur was appointed to Boulogne, part of the small dispersed work in which the WMMS was engaged in France. He prepared with seriousness, reading French literature and attempting to improve his skills at spoken French. Private correspondence reveals that he was critical of preachers from the Channel Islands whose imperfect French marred their effectiveness in France. They spoke French 'far worse than Welshmen speak English', Arthur complained.[41] He also applied himself to a devotional study of the Bible, believing that though he had already acquired a reputation for wisdom and preaching he still had much to learn:

> May God teach me! The Ministry becomes ... more and more solemn. Souls, souls, souls are before me; my heart melts; why have I not lived, prayed, preached more in sight of the cross and of the judgment? I earnestly desire to be filled with the Spirit.[42]

What he longed for most was 'a greater concentration of mind upon the things of God'. Wider studies and activities were not, however, neglected. He gave a lecture in London on Islam, and in 1847 he completed his first book, *A Mission to the Mysore*. This was published initially in instalments in successive numbers of the WMMS magazine.

At the Wesleyan Conference of 1847 Arthur was appointed to Paris. He had felt under-employed in Boulogne and welcomed the move. As he confided to Rigg, however, his preference was to serve India in some way. This implies that he was being considered at the time for appointment as a Secretary of the WMMS, since it is unlikely he would have been well enough to return to India. In his congregation in Paris, he shared with Rigg, there would be Britons, Americans, French, Italians, Germans and Russians. He would attempt to develop the French work especially.[43]

Arthur's mobility at this stage seems in part to be an example of the itinerancy at work, the system whereby Methodist preachers are moved regularly within the church's strategy. It was also probably an indication of the church's uncertainty as to how best to deploy a man of his quality and indifferent health.

Arthur was in Paris from 1847 to 1849, an interested spectator of the decline of the monarchy, the February revolution, the ensuing conflict over socialism, and the final 'class war' of June 1848. A lecture by him in London in January 1849 was a shrewd and vivid account of the main events in Paris from a socially conservative standpoint, providing clear evidence of his grasp of the key issues. Taking account of the fact that the first overt acts of violence were nearly all committed by young people, he pressed home the challenge that to leave vast numbers of young people 'untaught and irreligious' in any society, was to invite disaster.[44] Even earlier, in May 1848, while events in Paris were still unfolding, his experiences illumined his address at the annual meeting of the WMMS:

> The regeneration of the world is now the cry of every man that possesses any love for liberty. 'Regeneration!' is ringing round the barricades of Europe ... But that which is demanded, that which man really wants, is that which God has commissioned us to carry him, – not the regeneration of political institutions, but the regeneration of men.[45]

It was an especially opportune moment to engage in mission throughout the world, Arthur declared. The times demanded sacrifice on the part of Christians, to achieve the moral and spiritual regeneration needed in the world. Always the advocate of world mission, Arthur spoke of the WMMS reaching out on all fronts, to nominally Christian countries, to the colonies and to the heathen.

Also in 1848, Arthur expressed regret that Rigg had not

accepted an opportunity to serve in Montreal. Had it not been for his own indifferent health, he confided to Rigg, he himself would have been strongly tempted to join his former Indian superintendent, John Jenkins, in Canada.[46] An unsuccessful attempt was made at the Conference of 1848 to have Arthur appointed as a fifth WMMS Secretary, with special responsibility for missionary promotion. This was resisted on the grounds that he was still needed in Paris, and that there was insufficient income to take on additional staff. Dr Benjamin Gregory, later to become the Connexional Editor for many years and a President of the Wesleyan Conference, strongly favoured the appointment. To him Arthur was ideally suited, being an outstanding orator 'with all the glow and . . . passion of a Grattan, and all his dignified and compressed argumentativeness'.[47] Arthur, despite continuing uncertainty, remained philosophical about his future. Whether he stayed in Paris, or was appointed to a circuit in Britain or Ireland, or went to the Mission House in London, he felt that 'it will be right' in the end.[48]

The year 1849 was a momentous one for Arthur. He was appointed to a circuit in London, Hinde Street. He delivered his important lecture on the French Revolution of the previous year. He also became involved in the bitter controversy which had been raging for some years within Wesleyan Methodism. Fanned by a series of anonymous Fly Sheets, a number of contentious issues was raised including church administration, the authority of ministers and the role of the laity, Wesleyan Methodism's policy on education, and, most sensitive of all, the 'London hierarchy' with Jabez Bunting as the central figure. Agitation gathered momentum through the 1840s and continued into the 1850s, splitting congregations and, as Arthur later acknowledged, threatening to tear the church apart. A third of the membership was lost with the formation of the United Methodist Free Churches in 1857.

Arthur spoke out on behalf of Bunting. This need not surprise us. Apart from the rights and wrongs of the controversy, Bunting had played a key part at crucial moments in Arthur's life. He had been accepted as a candidate for the ministry, and ear-marked for overseas service, during Bunting's presidency of the Irish Wesleyan Conference. He had studied at the college at Hoxton where

Bunting also presided. Bunting had been officially involved in Arthur's commissioning and valedicting for India. On Arthur's return to Britain, when his association with the WMMS was retained, Bunting was its senior Secretary. Arthur made a strong defence of Bunting's character and role in the church, in a biographical study published in the *Christian Times* in 1849.[49] In October the same year he delivered a stirring address at Brunswick Chapel, Leeds, a centre of the agitation. In this he turned to the advantage of missions the slogan from Bunting's opponents to 'Stop the Supplies', by which they had hoped to weaken Bunting's powerbase within the Missionary Society through the withholding of resources to the WMMS. Arthur argued that ordinary Methodists would follow their own instincts and would not be taken in by misleading press reports. Those lay people with knowledge of the WMMS would have confidence in its policies and administration, he claimed. At the present period of need and opportunity, giving should and would be greatly increased. Beyond the disputes of Wesleyan Methodists, he insisted, the only people favouring a cut-back in resources to the WMMS were opponents of missions. These included the Pope himself, Buddhist priests in Ceylon, slave traders in Africa, Brahmans in India, Chinese mandarins and Muslim leaders.[50]

Arthur's voice had been under strain prior to his departure to France. In the early months of 1850 it broke down, recovering sufficiently by the time of Conference for him to be appointed to another circuit in London, Great Queen Street. Thereafter, however, it was frequently too unreliable to allow continuous public speaking. After a year of broken service, his itinerant circuit ministry was effectively brought to an end in 1851. Despite concern about his health, Arthur married Elizabeth Ellis Ogle from Leeds in June 1850. It is significant that Dr Bunting officiated at the wedding.[51] Possibly Arthur's initial contacts with the Ogle family were through Methodist families in the north of Ireland and Leeds, who shared a common interest in the linen industry.

Arthur was appointed a WMMS Secretary in 1851. His knowledge, counsel, commitment and integrity were thus made available to the wider church and to missions in particular. He could only occasionally address large gatherings, often being unable to speak at length or with his former vigour, but his influence grew none the less. His travel, writings, and contacts with people in Britain, Europe and the United States gave him a vantage point from which to influence national and international thinking and events within Methodism and to some extent within other churches.

Although close to Dr Bunting, Arthur retained a degree of independence in thought and action. He was never a party man, choosing to exercise his own judgment as issues arose. For example, he had spoken at the Wesleyan Conference of 1850, in an atmosphere of continuing controversy and agitation, on behalf of the appointment of a committee to consider the state of the church and to seek measures for improvement. This clearly implied an acknowledgment that all was not perfect within Wesleyan Methodism. The initiative failed, but the following year a committee was appointed along similar lines. The committee's members were drawn from the senior, middle and junior ranks of the Wesleyan ministry, with arrangements made to consult the laity. Arthur and Rigg were two of its youngest members. Its proposals were accepted by the Conference of 1852, with only slight amendment.

In 1852 Arthur's biography of Samuel Budgett, a Bristol businessman, was published under the title *The Successful Merchant*. The following year he co-operated with two wealthy lay friends, one of whom was the son of Samuel Budgett, to launch the *London Quarterly Review*. This journal sought to provide informed comment on the events and literature of the day. It brought to fulfilment a hope Rigg had expressed to Arthur in 1849, that there would be a Wesleyan review in line with those in other denominations and in the aftermath of controversies in which the *Watchman* and the *Wesleyan Times*, both with Wesleyan connections, had taken different sides. The fact that Rigg's half-brother was the editor of the former, and Arthur was assisting the Connexional Editor, facilitated this development. It was not the policy of the *London Quarterly Review* to include the names of those who wrote articles, but many notable contributions appear to have come from Arthur's pen. In the early years these included articles on Ultramontanism (1853), the exhibition at Crystal Palace (1854), Methodism and the Established Church (1856), and Dr Bunting (1859).[52]

His appointment as a WMMS Secretary greatly strengthened Arthur's links with Ireland. He regularly attended the Irish Wesleyan Conference as a representative from the British Conference, and was invited to take part in special functions. In 1855 the Irish Conference launched a fund to strengthen Wesleyan Methodism, in an attempt to recover ground lost through emigration in the post-famine years. Arthur accepted an invitation to go to the United States of America to promote the fund, along with Robinson Scott, a senior Irish Wesleyan preacher. Despite a loss of impetus caused by Arthur's illness early in the visit, the delegation met with considerable success. Money was raised for educational programmes in Ireland, and for the recruitment and training of Wesleyan preachers. This was Arthur's first visit to America. Other visits took place in 1880 and 1891.

Arthur was elected a member of the Legal Hundred in 1856, the body to which was assigned the conduct of legal business of the Methodist Conference by Wesley's Deed of Declaration. Arthur's best known and most influential book, on the role and importance of the Holy Spirit and entitled *The Tongue of Fire*, was also published in 1856. It appeared in eighteen editions in three years, and was translated into many languages, coming to be regarded as a spiritual classic. It was published in America in 1857. Indeed it has been suggested that Arthur's views on revival and renewal, expounded in person during his visit to America in 1855 and in the pages of *The Tongue of Fire*, played a part in the gathering pace of revival in the United States.[53] How striking, therefore, that when news of revival in America influenced the course of events in Ireland, it was in Arthur's home parish of Kells that some of the first signs of awakening appeared. This in turn led to the Ulster Revival in 1859.

Ill health continued to be a problem, and after a further breakdown in 1856, Arthur was given unlimited leave of absence in the hope that he could resume full duties after a period of recuperation and change. Early the following year he set off with his wife on a tour, reaching Cairo in March. By April they had arrived in Jerusalem, and his voice which had been strong and clear in the desert air became hoarse again. He was therefore faced with the prospect of returning to Britain 'without confident expectation of being able to do public work'.[54] Letters home set their travels in a biblical context, and reported an incident in which they had an encounter with three armed and mounted Kurds.[55]

In June 1857 he reported to Rigg that his voice showed no signs of improving, coming under strain even in lively conversation. A further wave of speculation had arisen as to his future. His own view on various possibilities that were being mentioned was that he was unfit for circuit work, a position as editor might further damage his eyes, and he did not relish an appointment at Richmond, presumably to teach at the ministerial training college. He could of course be asked to remain at the Mission House. Perhaps in all the circumstances, he surmised, it would be best for him to be given another year off, to take stock of the situation. At any rate he would state his views 'plainly & strongly' to the authorities, and then abide by whatever decision they made.[56]

Arthur in fact stayed at the Mission House. It can only be assumed that it was ill health which prevented him from taking a leading part in urgent inter-church and inter-missionary society talks in the winter of 1857 to 1858, in response to the Indian Mutiny. He was, however, on hand at the Mission House with Elijah Hoole, to welcome and pray with a group of fourteen women who came together in December 1858. The meeting led to the formation of The Ladies' Committee for the Amelioration of the Condition of Women in Heathen Countries. Despite the contrast in the title between 'ladies' at home and 'women' overseas, the committee was neither smug nor condescending. It burned with passion to save the souls and open the minds of women throughout the world, and was the formal beginning of many initiatives by Wesleyan women towards full and creative involvement in world mission through the WMMS.

Arthur's concern for the work overseas did not blind him to needs much closer to home. He took a practical interest in the building of the Wesleyan chapel at Bayswater, and rejoiced in the ministry of his friend Dr Morley Punshon in Hinde Street and Denbigh Road. At the Wesleyan Methodist Conference of 1859, Arthur came out forceably in favour of a concentrated form of ministry in urban areas while others argued for a unified pattern of circuit ministry throughout the connexion. The background to this debate was the continuing response to the census of 1851, the results of which drew attention to what the Wesleyan Conference described as 'the heathenish population of our large cities'. Arthur was a keen observer of the Ulster Revival, and expressed the hope in a series of pamphlets that revival would be widespread and continuous.

In 1860, for reasons of health and because of policy differences over the Wesleyan mission schools in Ireland, Arthur tendered his resignation as a Secretary of the WMMS. This, however, was withdrawn the following year.[57] Arthur visited Italy in 1860, a time of political ferment in that country. His *Italy in Transition* gave wide circulation to his observations on the political and religious developments in the country, as separate duchies and principalities moved towards a united Italy in the face of Austrian and Vatican opposition. Much of the book is taken up with the views of ordinary Italians with whom Arthur entered into casual conversation. In his report to the WMMS, he said that he had found evidence of a widespread dislike of popery and considerable interest in other forms of Christianity. There were no press restrictions in many areas, and Protestant literature printed in Italy was readily available. Evangelical initiatives had already taken place in Turin, Genoa and Florence. In his view it was time for a Wesleyan initiative. Two missionaries were designated in 1861, the beginning of Wesleyan Methodist witness in Rome. Arthur's growing familiarity with the Italian language and its literature, and his interest in political as well as religious developments, meant that he remained a keen observer of the power struggles within Italy. An informed article in the *London Quarterly Review* summarized political developments in the country from the end of the Crimean War to the strengthening of the Kingdom of Italy by the mid–1860s.[58] He paid particular attention to the Papacy's attempts to add to its influence through the publication of the Papal Syllabus and the Acts of the Vatican Council, including the decree of the dogma on Infallibility. Articles in the *London Quarterly Review* such as 'The Pope's Encyclical' (1865) and 'The Vatican and the Kremlin' (1866), prepared the way for the elaborate volume *The Pope, the Kings, and the People* (1877), on the first Vatican Council.

During the American Civil War Arthur contributed typically informed and forthright articles in the *London Quarterly Review* and other places. In opposition to the cotton interest in Lancashire and the British press, including *The Times* and the *Daily Telegraph*, he took the side of President Lincoln and of the Northern States, affirming that what was at stake was not the occupation of new tracts of land by the people of the South, but rather the ill effects of slavery on new states. American slaveholding, Arthur maintained, was 'the most highly organized system of living by violence' yet seen.[59] Lincoln's struggle was therefore interpreted by him as 'a noble, humane, hazardous warfare, in a holy and Christian cause'.[60] This stand, and a favourable article on the President following his assassination, greatly raised Arthur's profile in America. An honorary MA from Dickinson College, Pennsylvania, is an indication of the regard in which he was held in the United States.[61]

Arthur's criticism of the British press over the Civil War in America acquires greater significance when it is recognized that it appeared in print in the month in which he became President of the Wesleyan Methodist Conference. After making the point that people possess an extraordinary capacity to persuade themselves that the righteous position in disputed matters is the one that happens to coincide with their own particular prejudices, he continued:

> There exists a tacit compact between the most influential part of the nation and the most influential part of the press: the upper strata of English society undertake to believe whatever the said part of the press – the *Times* at its head – shall peremptorily affirm to be a matter of fact; and the *Times* undertakes the precise amount of suppression of some facts and skilful distortion of others which may flatter the prejudices without alarming the consciences of its readers ... There is a refined, a moderate, a gentleman-like, an apparently off-handed treatment of facts, so as to make them tell on the side to which the reader already leans.[62]

Arthur saw the same factors at play in the role of the press in other public controversies in which he became involved, notably the Irish Home Rule question. There is a familiarly modern ring about Arthur's stance. Compare, for example, the allegations about 'a Tory-dominated press' in Britain.

Responding to what he regarded as biased and inaccurate coverage in the British press of an uprising of black people in Jamaica, including again the *Daily Telegraph* and *The Times*, Arthur made a forthright speech in Folkestone in 1865. This was later published. Arthur pointed out that Christians had a special obligation to stand with the oppressed,[63] and that those who had rioted were reacting against harsh and unjust treatment. It was surprising that they had not used force earlier. Contrary to reports in the press, missionaries had exercised a restraining and responsible influence. Actions taken to suppress the riot had, however, gone far beyond what was justified. His final comments were particularly forceful, revealing an uncompromising commitment to the unity of humankind and against racist attitudes. Everyone, he declared, had the right 'to wages when he works, a hearing when he complains, and to have the truth told of him whether as an individual or a race'.[64]

In 1866, Arthur was elected President of the Wesleyan Methodist Conference. At forty-seven years of age he was the second youngest man to have become President. This was an acknowledgment of his many gifts, and it repaid the confidence shown in him during frequent periods of ill health. His opportunities for reflection and for travel abroad, largely necessitated by sickness, had brought dividends.

Inevitably, concern was expressed over Arthur's ability to withstand the rigours of the presidency, and hints were given at the Conference over which he presided that he might be relieved of some aspects of administration. He, however, resisted such a move. 'I shall go on till God stops me', he declared.[65] In fact his health held up remarkably well during the year. Reports of his preaching referred to his clear voice as well as the challenging content of his sermons. Also impressive was his grasp of committee procedure and his ability to steer meetings through their business, areas of work in which he did not have a great deal of previous experience. Main concerns in his presidential year were consistent with the rest of his ministry, including an emphasis on evangelical truths, social and evangelistic witness, and growth in the spiritual life.

College President (1868 – 1871)

At the Wesleyan Methodist Conference of 1867, in which Arthur's term as President came to an end, a strong plea was made by the Irish representatives for Ireland to be given the benefit of his leadership in launching the proposed Methodist College in Belfast in 1868. Secondary education had been available in Dublin under Wesleyan auspices from the 1840s. With economic growth and other developments in and around Belfast, it had become necessary to extend such facilities to the northern part of the country as well. A college had therefore been planned to provide education for ministerial and lay students, including preachers' children. The request to release Arthur to head up the new college was keenly debated within the Wesleyan Conference, many leading figures including Rigg and Punshon, both close friends of Arthur, opposing it. When the vote was taken, a majority came out in favour. Arthur himself took no part in the debate, his silence being interpreted by many as a sign of agreement. Those who knew him best, however, were sure that he would have preferred to remain in London with his young family, living in familiar surroundings and doing work to which he was accustomed and committed.[66]

From the outset, the new institution, composed of both a 'college' and a 'school', aimed at providing education for boys from the earliest stage of schooling to the completion of a university degree or entrance into business life. The school was divided into preparatory, intermediate and upper sections, with places for day and boarding pupils. The college was for candidates for the ministry (with biblical studies, theology and practical aspects of ministry) and for lay undergraduates at the nearby Queen's College (later Queen's University), providing religious education for all and accommodation as required.

Arthur must have approached his new assignment with a degree of uncertainty, even apprehension. It takes little imagination to appreciate some of the unease he would have felt. He was to be President (or Principal) of a new multi-purpose educational institution. There would be a theological tutor in the college, Dr Robinson Scott who had accompanied him to America in 1855. Dr Robert Crook, who had already been Headmaster of the Wesleyan institution in Dublin, was to be Headmaster in the school. Misunderstandings and tensions were almost bound to arise over roles and respective areas of responsibility. Also, although deeply rooted in Wesleyan Methodism, Arthur's direct knowledge of the tradition within Ireland was largely confined to the few years following his evangelical conversion as a teenager in the remote west of the country, and to visits as a senior Wesleyan figure from Britain. Belfast, however welcoming, was bound to be unfamiliar after London, far removed from people, places and institutions he valued and had grown to love. Most serious of all, despite a keen and informed interest in education, he had little experience of formal teaching. This was a major disadvantage for one accustomed to prepare himself with great thoroughness for each task. It also meant that many of the skills he had already acquired would be largely under-used.

There were of course positive points. Whatever hesitation Arthur, and perhaps some others, may have felt about his suitability, his fellow Wesleyans in Ireland had made their official position clear. He was a 'loan' to Britain and the world church whom they now wished to re-call, at least for some years, because of his known abilities, high standing, and breadth of vision and experience. His was a prestigious appointment which, the authorities believed, would greatly help in establishing the new school and college. For Arthur too there were compensations. He would be back in the land of his birth, and be in a position to repay something to the church to which he owed so much. He was also to be intimately involved with the first years of an institution the dream of whose creation he had long shared with others, and whose founding principles he thoroughly approved. These principles included a broad approach to education, with commercial subjects such as bookkeeping and the principles of commerce respected alongside literary and classical subjects. Full recognition was also given to the importance and practice of Christian virtues. In the years prior to the opening of Methodist College he had been active in securing financial and other support. For example, he had helped to arrange that the whole of the Irish contribution to the Jubilee (1863) Fund of the WMMS was ear-marked for the college, and he had served for a period as chairman of its Committee of Management when things were at the planning stage. His association with the institution certainly enhanced its status. One example is the way in which his inaugural address at the opening in August 1868 received wide and favourable coverage in the press.[67]

Arthur's private correspondence provides fascinating glimpses into the college's early life. In August 1868, he expressed a mixture of frustration and appreciation at the personal arrangements for his family and himself. He still had no shelving for his books though other matters had been attended to well if somewhat belatedly.[68] In October he reported to Rigg that they had eighty boys in the school section and four students in the college section. As Queen's College was about to commence a new academic year, it was possible that the numbers in the college section would rise.[69] By December numbers had increased to ninety-seven boys and eight students. Significantly a start had also been made on 'ladies classes' which promised 'fairly'.[70] Three years later there were three hundred pupils 'of all sorts'.[71]

His family's record of ill health during this period makes sad reading. In October 1868, two of his daughters had been ill, as had members of the domestic staff. To everyone's discomfort 'the water pipes, gas pipes, chimnies etc etc keep going wrong'. This, he supposed, was not unusual in a new house.[72] In December he referred to 'much illness' affecting each of the children in turn.[73] By January his own throat had begun to trouble him again, forcing him to take a few days' rest by the sea at Rostrevor.[74] After Conference that year, he was unable to speak at public meetings with the exception of missionary events at which he could manage to say a few words. In April 1870, he shared with Hoole that his throat had 'long been sadly out of sorts', making it difficult for him to preach even once a week in small chapels. His family was faring no better, having to spend several months by the sea.[75] Their darkest hour came late in 1870 when their eldest daughter died of typhoid. This sad loss cast a long shadow over their stay in Belfast, and remained a bitter memory.[76] By June 1871, when Arthur's period at the college was nearing its end, his throat was troubling him more than for the previous ten years. He was forced to give up preaching and class-work completely, and compelled to live outside the college. Next connexional year, he confided in Rigg, he would require 'entire rest'.[77]

One of the greatest problems with which he had to reckon was the narrowness of outlook among some of the people around him. The contrast with London could scarcely have been greater. In Belfast, he confided to Rigg, concerns tended to be petty, and opinions, though expressed sharply, were provincial.[78] It was therefore difficult to find time or kindred spirits with whom to consider wider questions. His frustration became particularly acute when he felt too far removed from the centre of things to influence Wesleyan Methodist thinking on national education. His, he recognized, was a minority view, but he argued it forcefully in correspondence, imposing great strains on his relationship with Rigg and other leading Wesleyans.[79] He also wrote to the press on aspects of the national debate on education.

Arthur's health largely determined how much he was able to do in Methodist College. When well, his activities were not restricted to administering, promoting and overseeing the institution. In December 1868 he was taking sixteen weekly classes.[80] By March 1871 he felt under so much daily pressure that there was little opportunity to become involved in wider issues outside the college.[81] In June of the same year ill health had forced him to abandon his 'little lectures'.[82] This is sufficient evidence to reject a claim that he 'taught none in the College in either departments' (sic).[83]

J.D. Foster, who entered Methodist College in 1870 and became a Methodist minister, provides an insight into Arthur's mode of discipline. No cane was used. Arthur talked to, and sometimes prayed with, offenders, and made them aware of the consequences of their actions. There was, Foster recalled, such an awesome atmosphere that 'the cane would have been a joyful alternative'.[84]

Arthur's term as President of Methodist College, punctuated by ill health and burdened by grief, had proved difficult and demanding. By its completion, however, Arthur and the college authorities were comforted by the knowledge that a good beginning had been made. The college today maintains high educational standards. Fully co-educational, it has over sixteen hundred pupils in the main school of whom approaching two hundred are in boarding departments for boys and girls. The college continued to be responsible for providing training for the Methodist ministry up to 1926, though this was organized on a separate site from 1919.

Honorary Secretary of the Missionary Society (1871–1888)

Arthur's links with the WMMS had been retained, at least on paper, during his period at Methodist College, and were expressed in the title 'Honorary Secretary'. On his return to London he made his home in Clapham, and continued to be regarded as an Honorary Secretary of the WMMS until his retirement in 1888. He held no other appointment, and in official listings of WMMS Secretaries his name normally stood after those of the General Secretaries. This arrangement gave him status in the final phase of his active ministry. It also recognized his indifferent health, in that no demands were automatically placed on him. Whatever contribution he was able to make at a particular time, depending on his physical condition, was accepted and valued. He was an infrequent attender at meetings, absented himself from the country at times in the interests of his health, and contributed most through informal contacts and publications. Stirring speeches and sermons were largely a thing of the past, on account of his weakened and unreliable voice. His eyesight was poor too, but not to the extent that he could not communicate through the written word. To achieve this, however, help was necessary. In the preface to his biography of the noted Irish Wesleyan evangelist, Gideon Ouseley, which was published in 1876, he pointed out that for essential reading he had now not only to use spectacles but also a 'large hand-glass, such as people employ in looking at photographs'.[85] His mind remained as alert and well-stocked as ever, enabling him to grasp issues and to advance views which always commanded respect and frequently won acceptance. The situation was made easier in that friends of long-standing, who knew his worth and limitations, were involved in the work of the WMMS. For example, the January meeting of its General Committee in 1875 was chaired by Dr Punshon as President of the Wesleyan Methodist Conference. Among others present were Dr Rigg, Sir Francis Lycett and William M'Arthur, MP, all close friends.

Arthur's London home became a meeting place for leading Irish and English Protestants of various denominations and political parties. In the 1870s, they met partly to resist Gladstone's proposal to give grants to the Roman Catholic University in Ireland, set up under papal authority in 1854, which developed into University College, Dublin. Influential Fellows of Trinity College, Dublin, and representatives of Ulster Protestantism consulted in Arthur's home, and put before English Nonconformists facts and arguments in opposition to Gladstone's proposals. They also turned their attention to the Home Rule question. Arthur's pamphlet, *Shall the Loyal be Deserted and the Disloyal set over Them?* (1886), enjoyed a wide circulation.

In 1880, Arthur attended the General Conference of the Methodist Episcopal Church in America as a representative of the British Wesleyan Conference. This enabled him to take part in discussions on both sides of the Atlantic about arrangements for the proposed first Methodist 'Oecumenical' Conference, the precursor of the World Methodist Council, which took place in London in 1881. Arthur read the opening paper at the first plenary session, entitled 'Methodism, a Power Purifying and Elevating Society'. Other themes on which he contributed were the deployment of ministers in cities, holiness, Sunday observance, informed Methodism, education, women in mission, patriotism, co-operation in mission and voluntary church union.[86] Arthur returned to the United States in 1891, to take part in the second Methodist Ecumenical Conference. His sermon, read for him at the opening session because of his loss of voice, occupies more than twenty pages of the official report. Spelling out the church's mission, the sermon said of its scope:

> She was sent 'unto all the world' – no limit of territory; to 'make disciples of all nations' – no limit of race; to 'preach the Gospel to every creature' – no limit of caste, class, or condition, nor yet any limit of number until the last unit is reached.[87]

Arthur also wrote the introduction to the conference's report, as indeed he had done ten years earlier. In addition to chairing a session on the church and scientific thought, he contributed to a range of discussions including unity, inter-church co-operation, the need to hold together breadth and conviction, the laity and international arbitration.

Arthur's publications included *Women's Work in India* (1883), which had a direct bearing on the concerns of the WMMS.

Following an article on Spinoza in the *London Quarterly Review* (1879), his mind turned increasingly to current philosophies and their relationship to the Christian faith. This led to a series of publications. *On The Difference between Physical and Moral Law* (1883), was his Fernley lecture at the Wesleyan Methodist Conference, in which he argued the case for the existence of God from design. In *Religion without God* and *God without Religion* (1885–1888), originally published in three parts, he examined positivism, agnosticism and deism. In *On Time and Space, Two Witnesses for a Creator* (1887), he presented another version of the argument from design. These were brave attempts to undergird theism. Not surprisingly, however, they made only a limited appeal, many preferring the line taken earlier by Arthur in *The Tongue of Fire*, that the most convincing argument on behalf of Christianity is its power to transform life. 'The only real and effective evidence', he claimed there, 'is living men who have been regenerated.'[88]

Years in Retirement (1888 – 1901)

Arthur retired in 1888, fifty-one years after his acceptance as a candidate for the Wesleyan Methodist ministry. The early signs had not been such as to encourage hope of a long period of service, as Arthur readily admitted. Methodism had 'found' him, he acknowledged, 'away beyond all the bogs of Connaught on the shores of the Atlantic'.[89] When his case was being considered at the Irish Wesleyan Conference, it was suggested that he be sent to Armagh. Others took the view, however, that unless care was exercised, he might kill himself before his probation had been completed.

His wife took seriously ill in 1885, and died in 1888. She had been a great strength to him, maintaining a loving, secure and hospitable home. His sister, Anne Jane, had married James Lindsay who was a generous supporter of Methodist College. They built a holiday home, 'Lisnacrieve', overlooking the Mediterranean at Cannes, France, which they eventually made their permanent home. This was a favourite place of retreat for Arthur in times of poor health, where he attempted to re-build his strength. He inherited the property following the death of his brother-in-law and sister, and made it his home for the last ten years of his life. The climate there suited him perfectly. His main regret was that in Cannes he was far from Methodist people and chapels, although he was able to attend a Presbyterian church. Visits by friends were greatly treasured.

In November 1900, Arthur took ill in Dijon with 'pulmonary catarrh', and on his return home he developed herpes on the neck. In a letter to Rigg, Mary Arthur wrote that on account of his accustomed vitality the doctor believed he had 'a better chance than most of recovery'.[90] This was a tribute to Arthur's spirit and lively mind. He died peacefully on 9 March 1901. He had been having periods of unconsciousness which became longer and more frequent, but in lucid moments he asked for and read his English and Hebrew Bibles, quoting texts and verifying references. Nor did he feel it incongruous, after reading the Bible, to ask for *The Times*.[91] It is fitting that Arthur, whose association with places in Ireland connected with Patrick has been noted, should have spent his final years within sight of the island, Lérins, where Patrick is said to have studied for some years prior to returning to Ireland.[92]

Arthur had been born three months before Queen Victoria, and died six weeks after her. Significantly, one of his last publications was a leaflet entitled *The Twentieth Century, in the View of Mission Work and Workers*. He was a staunch defender of evangelicalism and of Wesleyan Methodism, who encouraged co-operation and union between those of like mind. His position in politics and religion was normally conservative and always well thought out, which accounts for his strength of conviction and preparedness to argue his point of view without compromise. A product initially of Ireland and of Wesleyan Methodism, his influence came to be felt in the wider world and church.

2

Wesleyan Methodist

A teenage convert to Methodism in rural Ireland who later travelled widely and moved in influential social, political and religious circles, William Arthur remained a convinced Methodist and never lessened his commitment to the movement in which he was spiritually awakened. Involvement in Wesleyan missions and overseas visits made him familiar with the denomination in many parts of the world, and enabled him to appreciate its place in the wider church and in Christ's mission. Methodists had no need to fear comparison with any other branch of the church, he believed. Given their short history, he argued, it was remarkable what had been achieved through them.

Wesleyan Methodist confidence at this period has to be seen against the background of a persistent Anglican assumption that the Church of England represented the true and only church. As Henry Rack has pointed out, some Wesleyans 'regarded their doctrines, institutions and peculiar virtues with a self-confidence which to the modern observer verges on the complacent'.[1] This was undoubtedly reflected in Arthur, but at the same time he was not blind to some of the movement's faults.

Methodism claimed that its doctrines were based on the revelation of God in the scriptures. It affirmed the apostolic faith and accepted the fundamental principles of the historic creeds and of the Protestant Reformation, all of which enabled it to cherish its place in the Catholic Church. Arthur regarded Methodism's catholic nature as a guarantee of breadth in its understanding of the church, and as a factor which facilitated openness towards other traditions. Roman Catholicism, however, he felt to be a special case, a position which is examined later. It would be easy, he wrote, for those who took their religion seriously to become narrow. Wesley, however, provided a better model in that he was intense about religion without being narrow, drawing on the universal church in his spirituality and working for the renewal of the church in its widest sense. Methodism possessed 'no patent to protect it from decay' or regression, claimed Arthur. Instead of denying salvation to those who did not agree with them on all particulars, Methodists should take care to maintain a clear, positive faith. This would qualify them to meet and share with other Christians without fear or favour.

Arthur's view of the catholicity of Methodism, and his conviction that, despite different emphases, Protestants were essentially one, led him to resist strenuously a tendency on the part of some Christian leaders in the colonies to introduce divisive issues such as the comparative claims of Episcopal and Presbyterian forms of church order and ordination. Complaining of 'little and restless minds' which led people to split hairs, he commented that such a tendency posed a threat to the mission of the church:

> Can anything be more humbling than that a number of educated men should be found tearing up communities which are just emerging from barbarism, by discussions on ecclesiastical subtleties, respecting which even the bench of Bishops is not agreed? For the peace of the colonies, and the credit of religion, it is most earnestly to be hoped, that the election to colonial mitres will in future fall on men who have some higher view of their duty, than to suppose it is a mission of exclusiveness.[2]

The nature and primacy of Christian love was a major influence drawing Christians together, according to Arthur:

> If I cannot love except where the individual is the reflection of myself, either my political self, my theological self, or my ecclesiastical self, then I have no love like the love of my Redeemer ... To entitle a brother to your fullest affection, it is enough that he be conformed to Christ, though he be not conformed to you. The points of dissimilarity may be real, and of consideration. We need not deny their reality, nor underrate their importance. But when real differences are acknowledged we must judge how far they are to affect our love, and our manifested union.[3]

Yet there was a right way and a wrong way to promote union. Union through coercion or uniformity had to be strenuously resisted, Arthur believed.

In 1856, union between Methodists and Anglicans was unilaterally proposed by a committee of Anglicans. Initially given broad terms of reference, namely to consider what measures could be taken to promote union between the Church of England and other Christians 'not at present in active communion with her',[4] the committee early decided to focus its attention on Methodism, because of the special nature and history of the relationships between the two churches. When, however, the committee next turned its attention to how union could be restored between the two bodies, it soon concluded that because of differences over episcopal ordination union was not at that time practicable. Instead of abandoning its work, as Arthur clearly believed should have been done, the committee became 'a project of aggression', in his words, and ceased being 'a project of union'.[5] This was done by attempting to win over individual Methodist ministers and laypeople, on a basis which would have required the rejection of vital aspects of Methodism and an acceptance of a high Anglican view of episcopacy. In these circumstances Arthur deeply feared the loss of catholicity. This, he argued, would undoubtedly be the consequence if by joining the Anglicans some Methodists abandoned continuing Methodists and withdrew from Presbyterians, Congregationalists, Baptists and others. It was too high a price to pay. Schism on a wide front would be the outcome of union on a narrow front, and would lead to 'a breach of catholicity'.[6] Methodists did not claim to be the whole church of Christ, but they did regard themselves as within Christ's church, neither inferior nor superior to others. They were indebted to many branches of the church, and sought to be of service to the whole Body of Christ.

On the question of episcopal ordination, Arthur repeated the view which he held was that of Wesley that until the reign of Elizabeth I the Church of England had not insisted on its necessity. He also reiterated the belief that in the ancient church and in scripture, local presbyters were bishops. Methodists had no objection to a diocesan form of episcopacy 'as an ecclesiastical arrangement',[7] Arthur argued, but they did not believe that a higher order of clergy was created through additional ordination for presbyters. The position within the Church of England prompted a familiar attack by Arthur:

> The prevalent doctrine of the Church of England on the subject is looked upon (by Methodists) as an unwholesome graft from an evil stock; or as an innoculation from the diseased body of Rome, poisoning the system of the English Establishment, and leaving it subject to periodical attacks of Romish fever, followed by cold fits of rationalism, as at this day. It is, in their view, the most glaring infraction of catholic unity existing in any part of the Reformed Church, the greatest permanent danger to our national Protestantism, the sorest cause of internal plagues in the Establishment, the only fulcrum, – but one ever trustworthy, – on which Rome can rest her lever for disturbing the ecclesiastical mind of this country. Every Methodist who bows his head for re-ordination in deference to this doctrine, deliberately disowns all Christendom but the Church he is then adopting, – deliberately sanctions a divisive figment; and the day will never come when the Methodists, as a body, will be prepared for a proceeding so incompatible with fraternal respect for all the non-Anglican Churches in the world.[8]

Arthur was quick to add, however, that those whose only ordination was Anglican cast no reproach on other churches. In discussing Wesley's right to ordain, and in comparing Wesley with his contemporaries, Arthur was unrestrained:

> In the eighteenth century, there was no such Bishop as John Wesley, – a Bishop in right, a Bishop in fact, a Bishop in spirit, a Bishop in works, a Bishop in fruits, sound in doctrine, uncorrupt in living . . . reviled by the world, rejected by the Church, blessed by tens of thousands of converted sinners, – if ever man trod the soil of England who was entitled to call labourers into the Lord's vineyard, it was he.[9]

Some denominations have regarded themselves in different contexts as bridge-churches, holding the middle ground between the positions (perhaps extreme and exclusive) held by other churches. Anglicans, for example, have thought of themselves as providing a *via media* between the Reformed and the Roman Catholic traditions. Arthur saw Methodism fulfilling this role when, in his words, it avoided the extremes of Calvinism and semi-Pelagian Arminianism by affirming God's universal love without teaching man's merit or ability independent of God's Spirit; and by teaching salvation by grace alone though faith alone without the need for reprobation.[10]

In another sphere too he thought of Methodism as occupying the middle ground. Since the time of Constantine, when the church surrendered its independence and accepted from the state, wealth, recognition and civil power, some churches had been subservient to the state, some had attempted to achieve and sustain a dominant position over it, and some had opposed those churches which entered into a form of alliance with the state. Methodism, according to Arthur, followed none of these patterns. It had no dispossession to avenge, no lost ground to make up in the race for ascendancy, and no rivalry of civil eminence to sustain. Methodism arose, he wrote, 'without a congenital secular ambition, without a congenital political pliancy, without a congenital ecclesiastical grudge'.[11] The movement was respectful of the law and of the throne, and was jealous of its independence of state control. Its continued life proved that churches could grow without state aid and need not use their strength to attempt to undermine the privileges of other churches. Methodism, Arthur argued, should distance itself from Nonconformist attacks on the Church of England:

> The moment they become grievance-mongers, they would cease to be Methodists. Their business on the earth is to spread scriptural holiness . . . Once embarked in a career of Church politics, the spirit necessary to sustain their mission must die. They have counted the cost; they cannot hold on their present course without receiving blows on both sides; but, if the price of being 'the friends of all and the enemies of none' be, that they must expect enemies in all and friends in none . . . their minds are made up, the price is to be paid.[12]

The President of the Wesleyan Conference underlined in 1868 that Methodism provided a *via media* between Anglicanism and Dissent, but as the century advanced Methodism aligned itself increasingly with Nonconformity, partly in reaction to the Oxford Movement and Anglo-Catholicism.

Traditionally Methodism has recognized the importance of mission and evangelism, as its zeal for outreach at home and overseas bears witness. This will be taken up in detail later, but it is appropriate to note it here. Arthur referred to mission as 'the best of causes',[13] in which the whole church and each individual Christian had a part to play. Evangelism and social action were both involved, as was apologetics in which an attempt was made to respond to attacks on the Christian faith by philosophers and scientists. To Arthur, mission at home and overseas belonged together, each dependent on and contributing towards the other. Calling people to faith in Christ, and enabling them to grow in fellowship with others, were notes he constantly sounded:

> (Methodism) rose to 'National importance and world-wide influence', not by courting either the noble and learned on the one hand, or the populace on the other; but by bringing to every class alike the message of Christ, the Saviour from sin, the Saviour for all, the Saviour now, the Saviour to the uttermost.[14]

It was John Wesley himself who claimed that Methodism had been raised to spread 'scriptural holiness'. Wesley taught that God can remove sin from believers – sin in the sense of 'a voluntary transgression of a known law which it is in our power to obey'[15] – so that they are motivated solely by God's love. 'Christian perfection', 'entire sanctification', 'perfect love' and 'scriptural holiness' were closely related terms used by Wesley to provide slightly differing perspectives on this doctrine and experience. Because it is a work of grace received through faith alone, sanctification could be instantaneous, to be attested by the inner witness of the Holy Spirit. Yet it was not to be equated with the static state of 'sinless perfection', a concept which Wesley rejected. Understood in terms of an uninterrupted, dynamic love from God – between the believer and Christ, and from the believer to God and humanity – sanctification was also viewed by Wesley as progressive. Wesley's ambiguity at this point, his ability to hold in balance two understandings of holiness as crisis and process, was not matched by all who followed him.[16] Some highlighted the element of aspiration, and placed the emphasis on growth. Others stressed the element of experience, and urged that holiness was a gift to be received and confessed. In this latter approach, the importance of growth before and after the experience needs to be recognized.

Two modern scholars differ with regard to Arthur's position on this issue. J. Munsey Turner locates him among those who taught that entire sanctification was a gift to be received in a moment of awareness.[17] Arthur's prayer as President at the Methodist Conference in 1866, that God's love would be perfected in him, and his charge to ordinands a year later, that they should first lead their people to salvation and then to 'full salvation', adds support to this interpretation.[18] D.W. Bebbington, on the other hand, places Arthur in the other 'school'. Indeed Bebbington argues that Arthur watered down the teaching of Wesley on this subject, which Bebbington understands primarily in terms of gift, partly in an endeavour to commend Wesleyan Methodism to other churches. No evidence is produced to support this, and it does not accord with other instances in which Arthur, without undermining Methodism's catholicity, did not hesitate to draw attention to, and defend, its distinctive emphases.[19] That two such able scholars could come to conflicting conclusions on Arthur's position well illustrates a point made elsewhere. Arthur was not a systematic theologian. His views at times make classification difficult. They may not always have been consistent, and were not expressed in rigid terms.[20]

Holiness, declared Arthur at a convention in 1875, opened the way for conversions, since transformed lives attracted others to Christ. Conversion, for its part, produced candidates for holiness. Referring positively to meetings being held in Switzerland around that time by Pearsall Smith, a prominent holiness preacher from America, Arthur drew attention to the criticism in some quarters that it was 'nothing but Methodism'.[21] Methodism in its original form, he argued, was not more marked by a concern for justification by faith than for sanctification by faith, and many who shared its teaching on justification rejected it on sanctification. Admitting that there were different understandings of the nature of, and the means of attaining, sanctification, Arthur urged that a person could be sanctified in an instant but that this did not preclude the need for growth:

> The act whereby our Lord changed our diseased though not dead souls, into the very likeness of His own mind, may, like that whereby He will change our vile body into the likeness of His own body, be done in a moment – in the twinkling of an eye. But the living which follows that imparting of life will be one eternal development; the action which follows that restoration to soundness will be a career onward and onward, day without night.[22]

Methodism's vocation, Arthur maintained on another occasion, was to pursue and commend holiness:

> Seek national importance and you will lose it; seek only to spread Scriptural holiness throughout the land and you will bless the nation, and give the nation cause to bless God for you.[23]

Arthur regarded holiness as social in two senses, referring to the spiritual growth of people who met in fellowship with others and to its essentially practical nature. Jesus' holiness, Arthur maintained, was not other-worldly. It had been expressed in the routine duties of life for thirty years prior to the commencement of his public ministry. 'Holiness in common work' was 'the grandest of all holiness'.[24] In the eyes of the Roman Catholic Church holiness was experienced only by the few, most of whom were celibate and remote from the pressures of every day life. By contrast, in the light of Pentecost, holiness was available to all who had faith, and was relevant to the whole of life:

> The most dangerous perversion of the Gospel . . . is when it is looked upon as a means of forming a holy community in the world to come, but never in this. Nothing short of the general renewal of society ought to satisfy.[25]

Those empowered by the Spirit and holy in the New Testament sense had therefore the right and need to be concerned about such social evils as slavery, class alienation, child neglect, commercial fraud and poor housing. Within the church itself, Arthur claimed, financial and property matters were spiritual concerns. Unfaithfulness in those fields injured God's work.

'Religion', wrote Arthur in 1856, 'is a life to be lived in fellowship'.[26] In 1888, he submitted his comments on fellowship to a committee appointed by the Wesleyan Methodist Conference to consider church membership against the background of a growing debate about the place of the class-meeting. From the time of Wesley it had been the practice to direct spiritual enquirers into groups such as 'class-meetings', 'bands', and 'select bands', of which only the class-meeting continued into the nineteenth century. It emerged as the basic unit for evangelism and nurture, where those under conviction of sin found peace with God, and where believers grew in grace as they entered new depths of fellowship through the sharing of religious experiences. At no time, however, was the class-meeting above criticism. Wesley himself was required to defend it, and in the nineteenth century it came under increasing attack. Common criticisms included claims that its 'agenda' was too limited, that shared experiences tended to be repetitive, that social class differences created difficulties, and that class-leaders sometimes lacked vital leadership qualities. Other factors included the development of less formal prayer meetings, and, as the century progressed, the growing orientation around chapels with an increasing emphasis on public worship. As 'church' consciousness developed within Methodism, the appropriateness of earlier practices, however valuable, came into question. Expelling someone from membership of the Methodist 'society' for non-attendance at class-meetings, while they retained membership within the Church of England, was clearly not the same as expulsion after the link with the church had been broken. It seemed to some that Methodism was in danger of insisting on un-scriptural conditions of church membership. Others regarded classes differently, seeing them as a means of giving expression to Christian fellowship as outlined in the New Testament and as a practical way of nurturing people in the Christian faith.[27]

Arthur's submission in 1888 to the committee on membership was an eloquent re-presentation of aspects of traditional Methodist practice. He highlighted the manner in which people were received into Methodism on a profession not of conversion but of spiritual seriousness (that they desired 'to flee from the wrath to come'), and on the basis of a three-fold confirmation by members, a class-leader and a minister that they took their spiritual search seriously.[28] Through enlisting the support of the laity and testing the spiritual disposition of people in this way, it was underlined that they were not simply making individual professions. They were entering a family of believers who met regularly for fellowship. Such fellowship was vital for growth in the Christian life, and the fact that it continued to be valued after reception into membership could be viewed as a 'standing test' of spiritual health.[29] Arthur recognized fully the place of the Lord's Supper, which he referred to as 'the seal of membership'. Churches followed different practices with regard to admission to holy communion, including confirmation for some, the sanction of a kirk-session or a board of deacons for others, and confession in the Roman Catholic Church. Living fellowship determined Methodist practice:

> When the Methodists came to group themselves into churches, they were already provided with a well-defined form of qualification ... It consisted in a living relation to the living members of Christ's body. The society certified the candidate to the Church – certified him as one who, in coming to the table of the Lord, would not 'eat and drink damnation to himself' ... On the part of the recipient the Lord's Supper is the public profession and exercise of membership in the Body of Christ; and on the part of the Church it is the public seal set to his membership.[30]

The Methodist 'test of membership' – in terms of admission to, and continuance in, Christian fellowship – should be retained, he urged. It had ensured Methodist life and witness in the past, and could continue to do so. Earlier, in his presidential year, Arthur had claimed that the 'maintenance of fellowship with our brother Christians in meetings for mutual edification' was 'of the essence of a Christian Church'.[31]

In 1889, the committee on membership reported to the Wesleyan Conference. It recommended the retention of the traditional basis of membership, pointed out how fellowship in classes had been 'the very tissue and substance of living Methodism', recognized factors in society which had lessened the influence of classes, and recommended ways in which their effectiveness could be restored. Non-attendance at classes was not, however, to lead to a loss of membership, and reception services for new members were recommended. The need to cater for variety in religious experience, and for degrees of commitment, was thus recognized while 'fellowship' was still acknowledged as one of the characteristic features of Methodism.[32]

'The essential elements of church life', wrote Arthur 'are a godly ministry and scriptural doctrine'.[33] Methodists believe that their doctrines are faithful to God's revelation in the scriptures, so what can be said of ministry in the Methodist tradition? Arthur admitted that no system provided an infallible safeguard against the acceptance of unfit persons into the ordained ministry, or the continuance within it of people who started well but later proved themselves unfit. He none the less believed that the checks and balances contained within the Methodist tradition, including its view of the corporate nature of ministry, ensured high standards. The essential elements in this included a sense of call, the possession and testing of gifts, accountability and the anointing of the Spirit. Initially a person had to prove himself as a lay member. At the first stage he was accepted for the ministry after endorsement by other laypeople, and on the basis of knowledge of him by experienced ministers. Even after a solemn decision had been taken by ministers meeting in counsel together, acceptance was only under probationary conditions. On completion of a trial period, ordination took place but even this did not imply guaranteed long-term approval. Fitness for the retention of ministerial status was examined on an annual basis.

The system of itinerancy meant that ministers moved from one circuit to another after three years, and in principle any minister could succeed any other. The circuit system by which two or more ministers shared as pastors over the same societies (congregations) in a circuit, provided further checks. This system encouraged discipline through mutual oversight, and facilitated the building of morale and a sense of brotherhood within the ministry:

> That brotherhood is not one of rules, bonds, and cloisters, but one of nature and circulation, kindred birth, kindred

aims, kindred interests, and a flowing of the blood evermore from member to member, from part to part till, however various their forms and functions, the consciousness is never lost of the common life-stream running warm in the veins of all.[34]

Looking at the ministry in 'its purely Christian aspects', Arthur felt confident that no young Methodist minister would have 'reason to blush' if a comparison was made between his ministerial colleagues and the ministers of other churches.[35]

The itinerancy, Arthur claimed, made it essential that a church's health and progress should not be identified with the gifts and faithfulness of a particular minister. A preacher's predecessors all contributed to the richness of ministry, and their contribution had to be taken into account. The itinerant system also made the development of ministries for the laity imperative. Reference has already been made to the part taken by laypeople in accepting and nurturing new members, and in helping to assess the suitability of prospective candidates for the ministry. Methodism, Arthur pointed out, recognized many other contributions which the laity could make, including preaching, teaching, visiting the sick, gathering children from the streets, committee work, caring for property and engaging in outreach. The apostles did not distinguish between 'the teaching Church' and 'the learning Church' in a way that considered some to be merely passive members. 'The agents of the Church', he declared, 'include all her true members.'[36] For example, for laypeople to pray and preach in consecrated places might well be abhorrent to the Church of England, but to Methodists it was 'of the very spirit and essence of primitive Christianity'.[37] The admission of laymen to membership of the Wesleyan Conference in 1878 was a significant development in which Arthur played a key part. His contribution to the special committee appointed by the Conference to look into the matter, helped him to allay the fears of some, by arguing that lay representation could be viewed as the logical extension of previously approved policies and decisions. The fact that he was able to quote previously unreported words of the dying Jabez Bunting, which appeared to favour this approach, was particularly telling. 'My policy has been misunderstood', he claimed Bunting had said. 'My real policy was to secure the just rights of the people, or the proper representation of the people'.[38]

Arthur played a leading part in helping to create a consultative forum for world Methodism, which led in the twentieth century to the formation and development of the World Methodist Council. The General Conference of the Methodist Episcopal Church (MEC) in America took the initiative, calling in 1876 for a conference to be convened with representatives drawn from Methodist Churches throughout the world. After other branches of Methodism within America had been contacted, a letter was addressed to the British Conference of Wesleyan Methodism in 1878. A committee was appointed and in April 1880 it shared its thinking with Arthur, who was on the point of proceeding as a representative to the General Conference of the MEC about to be held in Cincinnati. After further discussions on both sides of the Atlantic, it was agreed to call the first Ecumenical Methodist Conference at Wesley's Chapel, London, in 1881, with four hundred delegates. Half were to be chosen by churches in Europe with their respective missions, and half by churches in America with theirs. The purpose was to consult on matters of common interest and concern in such a way as to allay, rather than to excite, controversy. Arthur drew attention to the way in which understanding was increased even in preparation for the Conference, as representatives from the two Methodist Conferences founded by John Wesley (in Britain and Ireland) met in committee with those of much more recent origin. Episcopal representatives met with non-Episcopal; black representatives, including some Africans, met with white; and Canadian representatives met with Americans. For the first time since 1844, when the main division took place in the American Church over the issue of slavery, bishops of the MEC, South, met at the same board with bishops of the MEC.[39]

The delegates assembled on 7 September 1881 representing twenty-eight denominations within the Methodist tradition. They came from England, Ireland, Scotland, France, Germany, Italy, Norway, Sweden, Switzerland, countries in Africa, India, China, Japan, Australia, New Zealand, Polynesia, the United States, Canada, and countries in South America and the West Indies. There were, however, limitations in representation, as Arthur observed. There was no African born and residing in Africa, nor any native Asiatic, American Indian or Polynesian. Only those were sent who could participate in the English language. It brought Arthur special pleasure that the representatives were invited to a public reception in the Mansion House by the Lord Mayor of London, the Right Honourable William M'Arthur, MP. He was a friend of Arthur's of long standing, whose roots also lay in Irish Wesleyan Methodism. Arthur played a significant part in the proceedings of the Conference, and delivered the major address at the first discussion session, on Methodism's influence in society.[40]

A second Conference was held in 1891 in Washington, DC, in the United States, with Arthur, although officially retired, again centrally involved. Although it was attended this time by five hundred people, Arthur was careful to point out continuing weaknesses in representation:

> No one represented the Methodists of Italy, or those of Scandinavia; no one those of the West Coast of Africa; no one those of the region of the Congo or of the Orange River or Transvaal. And what made the incompleteness of the representation more obvious was the absence of Christian brethren of the Polynesian, Hindu, Chinese, Japanese, Kafir, Zulu, and *African-born* Negro races. With the exception of a couple of French brethren, only the Teutonic and the *American-born* African races were present, and the English tongue was the sole speech heard in Conference.[41]

He hoped that by the time the next Conference was held in Washington, its sessions would 'resound with polyglot doxologies' from people of many more races.

In surveying the events affecting the mutual relations of Methodists in the interim between the Ecumenical Conferences of 1881 and 1891, Arthur regarded the union of Methodists in Canada in 1884 as the most important. Methodist co-operation and union were of special interest to him. In 1869 he had advocated union between the Wesleyans and the Primitive Wesleyans in Ireland, in a pamphlet entitled *Ought Not the Two Methodist Bodies in Ireland to Become One?* Union was eventually achieved in 1878. Though a committed Wesleyan himself, Arthur had enjoyed contacts with Primitive Wesleyans in the west of Ireland. He had discussed informally the possibility of Methodist union in Ireland with Dr Bunting in the late 1840s, and had begun to air his views on the matter since the mid–1850s.[42] Separation had taken place in 1818, largely because some felt that they should continue as a religious society within the Church of Ireland, to maintain a strong Protestant and evangelical witness, particularly in those areas in which Roman Catholicism was especially dominant. The Primitive Wesleyans were therefore opposed to the sacraments being made available within Methodism, a concession which the Wesleyan Methodist Conference in Ireland first granted to some northern circuits in 1816. Half a century of separation had lessened rather than increased the differences between the two bodies, Arthur argued in his pamphlet, with movement towards each other's position on holy communion and on lay representation in the annual Conference (which the Primitive Wesleyans practised). Both churches were 'true scions of the one stock', holding in common the essentials of faith, religious experience and church government, and sharing the same basic commitments and hopes.[43] He therefore urged them to seek union 'on a footing of equality and mutual confidence', neither body asking of the other what they could not concede.[44] Freedom of conscience should be allowed to those preachers who preferred not to administer the sacraments, and to those members who wished to receive the sacraments only in the Church of Ireland. Each body should respect the convictions of people in the other, and they should insist on uniformity only where established rule had marked a clear line. Arthur was convinced that union on this basis would lead to a stronger Methodist Church in Ireland. At the same time he was sensitive to the possibility that some Primitive Wesleyans might feel that in the event of union and on the eve of Disestablishment of the Church of Ireland, which took place in 1870, they should commit themselves to the Anglicans. Any who took that step should be assured of Methodist understanding and good will. Methodist union must not be viewed as a hostile act against the Church of Ireland. It would add greatly to the effectiveness of Methodism's evangelical witness both directly and indirectly through other churches, and in the future the spirit of Methodism would remain one of friendship towards others:

If I have one persuasion deeper than another it is that the value of the Church of England as a safeguard against Rome, when the latter is not kept down by the temporal arm, depends on her having at her side vigorous and holy nonconformist churches. Of these I believe Methodism tends most both to stir up the Church of England to good works, and directly to counteract the influence of Rome ... Where Methodism has never penetrated, the Church has seldom revived, and where it has, the Church has seldom altogether slumbered.[45]

Arthur's repeated emphasis on Methodist openness and friendship towards other Christian traditions did not indicate any lessening of his denominational convictions or commitment. In 1872, when sharp differences intensified over educational policy between Arthur and some of his closest friends, he was quick to dissociate himself from talk of 'party' and 'division' within Methodism. 'Methodism has made me all I am', he testified, and he could be joined to no other church. Their task, despite acknowledged differences, was 'to live together, work together, and die together'.[46]

3

Evangelical and Revivalist

D.W. Bebbington has noted four main characteristics of evangelical religion:

> *Conversionism*, the belief that lives need to be changed; *activism*, the expression of the gospel in effort; *biblicism*, a particular regard for the Bible; and what may be called *crucicentrism*, a stress on the sacrifice of Christ on the cross.[1]

All four feature prominently in the writings of William Arthur, as do others frequently associated with them including an emphasis on God's punishment of sin, a concern for evangelical unity, the promotion of 'Victorian values', and enthusiasm for mission at home and overseas.

Arthur's *Divinity of our Lord in Relation to His Work of Atonement*, which was published in 1885 in a series of 'present day tracts', is a traditional evangelical statement on sin and salvation at a time when some evangelicals were taking more liberal positions. Arguing from the writings of Peter, Paul and John, Arthur demonstrated that Christ was 'God manifest in the flesh', and that Christ did not simply fulfil a particular and limited mission but effected an atonement for the sins of the whole world.[2] He listed almost one hundred and fifty scriptural references in support of his argument. All people, Arthur maintained, were in their natural state enemies of God, having rebelled against God's will. Divine condemnation and punishment were therefore deserved. They in no way called God's mercy into question. Salvation for all was not inevitable, as some people argued. If it were, evil would be approved and damage done to morality. Salvation was indeed offered to all, not, however, on the basis of human effort or merit, but only on the basis of God's grace. Christ's propitiating death, initiated by God as Father, established the heinousness and blameworthiness of sin, showed God's righteousness as Judge, and enabled God to free the transgressor from condemnation:

> The question of how the guilty can be raised to the place and heritage of the innocent without undoing the foundations of all order and hope, could never be answered without an atonement. God sets forth Christ crucified, to show that even in this also He is just ... Those who believe in Him as dying, the just for the unjust, to bring us to God, view sin as abhorrent to a degree beyond what others ever do.[3]

God's anger towards the wicked and his punishment of sin were themes to which Arthur turned on other occasions. Aware that they had become unfashionable in some church circles, he firmly maintained that since Christianity took morality seriously, it could give sin no quarter. Mercifully, he argued, God's anger was forbearing rather than immediate, withholding punishment for a time and creating a period within which Christ appealed to human hearts and gave opportunity for repentance, pardon and reconciliation. Arthur rejected any suggestion that immortality was conditional on faith in Christ, with the persistently impenitent facing extinction rather than eternal punishment. As he proclaimed in a funeral address, all the dead – the wicked together with the just – live before God. Whereas the just were in a state of blessedness, the unrepentant faced a grim prospect of 'present woe ... coming wrath'. They were, Arthur feared, a 'lost community' separated from Christ and from those who through faith dwelt in him.[4]

In this connection Arthur contributed an essay to a volume published in response to Canon Farrar's *Eternal Hope* (1878). Farrar had argued against the concept of eternal punishment on behalf of a 'not Romish'[5] form of purgatory through which people would pass, after repentance, to heaven. Arthur accused Farrar of dealing superficially with such fundamental matters as the origin of evil, God's permission of wrong and God's toleration of those who acted contrary to his will. Farrar, Arthur claimed, had ignored the broad teaching of scripture, and had produced no scriptural evidence in support of his own position. In abolishing the concept of eternal punishment he had undermined morality, spilling out life through 'a thousand gurgling sluices'.[6]

Arthur regarded Bible knowledge as essential for discipleship, for personal and social morality, and for Christian doctrine. 'Everything great in religion proceeds' from the Bible, he wrote to Rigg:

> My Bible becomes richer and more attractive. I now love to pore over it, and endeavour to bore into it. Its truths and hopes are precious; I embrace them with a faith full of joy. God be praised for redemption![7]

He urged that, contrary to restrictions imposed in India, the Bible should be allowed to be taught in schools in the aftermath of 'the Mutiny'. This should not be compulsory, but 'where circumstances are favourable, and . . . *only to such pupils as may voluntarily attend*'.[8] This was necessary so that moral awareness could be developed in the hearts of the people. The Bible, Arthur believed, was by far the best means of conveying God's disapproval of such prevalent anti-social practices in India as oppression, extortion and bribe-taking.[9] In a sermon to candidates for ordination at the Wesleyan Methodist Conference in Britain in 1867, he declared that 'whatever you preach, let your doctrine be drawn out of the Scriptures'.[10] In discussing the importance of Bible-teaching in education, he affirmed in 1885 that 'the Bible and the strength and godliness of England have gone hand in hand'.[11] The lack of Bible-knowledge among Roman Catholics was of the utmost concern to Arthur and to other evangelicals generally. Somewhat tongue in cheek, Arthur observed in 1872 that, in keeping with his predecessors, Pope Pius IX quoted the scriptures in Latin. Of the three languages written on Jesus' cross, he commented, the Pope used that of his executioners rather than that of the Apostles (Greek) or the Prophets (Hebrew). Can indeed 'the infallible teacher of the Christian faith' read his Greek New Testament or his Hebrew Bible, Arthur speculated? On the whole though, 'we do not accuse Pio Nono much of quoting Scripture'.[12]

Sabbath observance was viewed as a matter of the utmost importance by Victorian evangelicals. In a highly detailed, and largely appreciative account of the exhibition in the recently opened Crystal Palace, Arthur expressed alarm lest it be opened to the public on Sundays. 'When Sunday becomes a day of pleasure, it ceases to be a day of rest',[13] he observed. Sunday, he argued, must be safe-guarded for rest, religious observance and the renewal of family life. The Sabbath was 'the most ancient and the most sacred civil right', every Briton's birthright, given by God and enshrined in the law for the physical and spiritual betterment of all.[14] It ensured, for example, that the seventh part of a working man's life was protected from labour. Sunday, Arthur argued, was a cornerstone of traditional values, catering for our need for reflection, worship and personal relationships. Arthur therefore felt confident in challenging his readers:

> We will accompany you wherever you please. Compare Sabbath-less cities, provinces, kingdoms, or republics, with Sabbath-keeping ones; and, without exception, you will find the balance of strong character, stable institutions, industry, virtue, wealth, and power, ever proportioned to the national respect for this all-influencing institution. What nation, so poor by nature, and so few in numbers, can compare with Scotland, even in spite of her whisky-drinking? What Republic is like America? what Colonies like those of England?[15]

Arthur inevitably perceived the spectre of Roman Catholicism hovering in the background. Wherever Protestantism retained or relapsed into 'the Romish Sunday', it fell short of its potential.

The People's Day, first published in 1855, was an appeal to Lord Stanley against his advocacy in parliament of 'a French Sunday', whereby he proposed the Sunday opening of museums and exhibitions. The pamphlet was re-issued in a sixth edition in 1885, when Lord Robert Grosvenor introduced a Sunday trading bill. Prominent among Arthur's fears was one that public houses and other places would also be opened in the vicinity of museums and exhibitions. 'A Sunday of mingled trade, religion, and dissipation', he warned ominously, 'is an engine of social corruption and of national insecurity, leading to the choice between anarchy or despotism.'[16] To the argument that from the cultivation of the arts, moral improvement might flow, Arthur acknowledged that the arts possessed value in polishing manners and in refining taste. Young people, for example, could benefit greatly from a guided tour of the Crystal Palace, their appreciation of good literature being greatly enhanced. These benefits would be lost, however, and the contrary consequences would be dire, if the arts were promoted at the expense of religious practice.[17]

'Nude statuary'[18] was another concern raised by Arthur in his article on the Crystal Palace. Nudity in sculpture or painting offended good taste, and prompted Arthur to point out that whereas the traditional characteristic of English vice was coarseness, people should equally be on their guard against 'elegant iniquity' such as was common elsewhere, for example at Versailles:

> Far more surely than coarse vice, it undoes a people . . . glides where it could not rush; confounds the sense of hateful and pleasing, bad and good; till men smile at crime, and the social structure comes down . . . Woe to England, when our people shall learn the art in which some of our neighbours are adepts, – the art of sinning sweetly, gracefully.[19]

A series of articles on juvenile prostitution in the *Pall Mall Gazette* in the summer of 1885, prompted a national outcry on issues related to sexual morality. Parliament was forced to rush through a Criminal Law Amendment Act, raising the age of consent from thirteen to sixteen years. A National Vigilance Association was formed, following a demonstration in Hyde Park, to ensure the enforcement of the Act.[20] One of the main issues to emerge was whether the sheer volume of debate, and the tone of some of it, had to some extent proved counter-productive. *The Times*, for example, spoke of 'a mischievous and degrading agitation', and commented:

> The purity of society is best promoted by individual purity of heart and mind, of thought and language. By the publication and discussion of obscene and disgusting details it can only be hopelessly retarded, and in many cases irretrievably destroyed. Already infinitely more evil has been done than the most sanguine of social reformers can hope to see cured by the passing of the Bill. Men were never made virtuous by Act of Parliament and never will be. But many an innocent mind has been corrupted by knowledge which it need never have acquired, and depraved by revelations of vice . . . it

would have never as much as dreamt . . . We shall soon need, not only a Bill for the amendment of the Criminal Law, but a Bill for the suppression of obscene agitation.[21]

This was the background to Arthur's 'Hush or Speak Out?', an article written as the Criminal Law Amendment Act was passing through Parliament. He counselled continuous vigilance against the resourcefulness of people capable of frustrating the law's operation. This, Arthur concurred, was not a time for 'coarse words, or extreme proposals'; nor, he countered, was it one for lapsing into silence or being inactive. Ministers of religion, journalists, magistrates, teachers and others in positions of influence should all speak out and strengthen the enforcement of the law. Contrasting the openness with which this Act had been introduced with the secrecy surrounding the Contagious Diseases Acts, Arthur declared:

> No concealment or pretence has covered the present enactment. Men know what it is and what it aims at. They know that it is a step towards making the law a terror to evil doers, rich or poor, titled or despised, princely or penniless. They know that it is a step towards shielding the young, the guileless, and the frail with the whole force of the national power . . . The sophism of silence must be torn to shreds. The conspiracy of silence must be counteracted by a steady conflict against crime, and a steady exposure of obscenity in action whenever detected, and of obscenity on paper, however graced and patronised.[22]

Some of Arthur's severest strictures were reserved for members of his own sex, for their tendency not to exercise restraint on the words and actions of other men. 'To cast upon woman the moral curbing of our sex', as well as holding them responsible for the moral elevation of their own, was 'unmanlike', he wrote. Fearless men should confront evil men on this issue in their clubs, colleges and even in parliament. He also pressed that there was a link, seldom recognized, between sexual crimes and crimes of violence:

> The proportion of cases of suicide, of infanticide, of murderous broil, and of deliberate assassination traceable directly or indirectly to offences against chastity is appalling . . . In

moving against the offence which is the fountain of all this class, we are not only manifestly fulfilling the laws of God and the precepts of Christ, not only serving in general our generation and humanity at large, but we are specifically preserving life, promoting health, and defending property.[23]

This public controversy had exposed a situation in which, claimed Arthur, the rich and powerful had been exploiting the poor and defenceless. Such crimes against the family had to be viewed in their true enormity. Good men should not hesitate to take sides with those who had been grievously wronged and against the evil-doers. In another context Arthur acknowledged that the law was not even-handed. A poor man who stole a coat, for example, was severely punished, whereas a 'gentleman' who swindled a family was 'daintily handled by the law'.[24]

Alcohol was another matter on which Arthur expressed himself forcefully. The drinking of (alcoholic) toasts was 'thoroughly out of fashion' during his presidential year.[25] He became Vice-President of the United Kingdom Alliance, the main political arm of the temperance movement, and declared himself in favour of the 'local option'. This affirmed the right to abolish or regulate the drink trade within a given locality. In view of what he regarded as the demoralizing influence of alcohol, Arthur urged that public houses should be closed if two-thirds of the people in a parish were in agreement. Those wishing to drink could go to a neighbouring parish to do so. Not all Wesleyans favoured teetotalism, however. Many pressed the need for moderation. Significantly, the first Wesleyan temperance societies, established locally after the creation in 1875 of a temperance committee for the church as a whole, included those who believed in moderation as well as total abstainers.

Arthur's commitment to evangelical principles, and his belief in the far-reaching effects of personal salvation, understood and applied, pointed the way forward when evil in its institutional forms was recognized and had to be countered. His social, economic, and political outlook was essentially conservative. Expressing the Christian faith in society was therefore understood mainly in terms of individuals being converted and engaging in humanitarian acts, while upholding traditional Christian values and accepting existing class and other differences. Slavery and racism were exceptions to this general approach, however. They could not be tolerated since they denied the essential humanity of their victims and failed to recognize that they too were people who had been created in God's image. The institution of slavery was viewed as sinful, and restricting missionary access to slaves erected barriers to missionary progress.

Arthur was alive to social inequality within Victorian society. To him the corrective lay in religious conversion and in enlightened capitalism, rather than in socialism and revolution such as he had witnessed in France. These latter led only to disruption and violence, when what was really required was moderate, controlled and gradual reform which took account of traditional differences and relationships. Writing of Britain, he argued that people were not, and never would be, equal, for example in height, strength, intellect and power over others. In a similar way, he insisted, 'the relation of master and men is natural, safe, manageable'.[26] Everyone, however, had an equal claim to 'liberty', presumably understood to include opportunity, as 'the only equality attainable'. It was therefore essential that those with power exercised it justly and fairly, and that everyone sought to provide for himself and his dependants:

> As a man enters on this world, he enters it the off-spring of the great Giver, and looking around on a whole race of brothers his inquiry should be, What service can I do, what part can I bear, what contribution can I give? ... not, What can I force all to do for me? And to a man in this mood of heart, nothing would be more unwelcome than to tell him, You are to be kept and cared for by the toil of others; you are to be a taker, not a giver. All of the Divine image that was in him would rebel – gently, generously rebel.[27]

Arthur admitted one exception to this, however. There would always be some people quite unable to provide for themselves, who also lacked relatives to support them. They, he accepted, required the care and protection of society. It remained true, however, that the worst thing you could do to a person was to 'pauperise' him, making him dependant on others.[28]

Capitalism was altogether preferable to other systems, Arthur argued, because it created wealth which in time would benefit everybody.[29] Employees, for example, would gain improved working conditions and enhanced wages. The influence of religion in this process was crucial, he maintained, steadily changing people's hearts, attitudes and relationships. Employees should be hard-working and reliable; while employers should support charities, and care for their workers. Inter-dependence was the ideal, coupled with an acceptance of the basic structure of society as it was. Arthur does not appear to have considered the moral issues raised by inherited wealth and privilege.

This is a familiar view of religion, seeing it as a benign influence for good which promotes moderate change, preserves harmony, and exercises social control. Arthur spelt it out in his lecture on the French Revolution:

> An unchristianised population is perpetual danger. But imbue the whole population with Christian principle, and they will not rashly burst into civil war; when they have rights to seek, they will be sought with calmness and dignity. Public order can have no security so effectual as the spread of real piety among the populace. Nor can the populace themselves have any security for their own liberties nearly so effectual. Let them not suppose that we would seek to make them religious in order that they might tamely submit to wrongs. No; but that they might irresistibly acquire rights. Any people that are liable to violent outbursts are, of necessity, exposed to military oppression ... A calm and pious populace would surely advance in all their rights; a passionate and irreligious populace bring oppression on their own heads.[30]

It is ironic that conservative French Roman Catholics of the period took a similar line on the place of religion, such beliefs helping to set the tone of charitable and devotional organizations in France in the 1850s and 1860s, as they sought to 'remoralize' the working classes.

There was a high expectation of revival in mid-nineteenth century Britain. Within Wesleyan Methodism, the controversial Irish-American, James Caughey, compelled people to take sides on the issue of revivalism. Originally from Portaferry in Northern Ireland, he had experienced an evangelical conversion in America, which led him to renounce the Calvinism of his youth and to join the Methodist Episcopal Church. Thoroughly grounded in the techniques and excitement of revival in America, he arrived in Britain in the early years of the railway, which facilitated his becoming one of the first full-time evangelists of the 'urban frontier'. He concentrated his efforts on such cities as Liverpool, Birmingham, Leeds, Hull and Sheffield between 1842 and 1846, claiming that in that period he had been instrumental in over twenty thousand conversions and in nine thousand people experiencing entire sanctification.[31] Although he operated largely in Methodist chapels, Wesleyan Methodism became sharply divided in its attitude towards Caughey. Some preachers offered him every facility and looked to him with great hope. Others, however, were deeply suspicious, and accused him of revivalist engineering through the use of 'decoy penitents'. The emotion his preaching generated aroused questions, though it was on a reduced scale when compared with the earlier 'Crazy' Dow, another Irish-American. The major difficulty with Caughey, however, was that he had come to Britain without credentials from American Methodism, and that he was operating without reference to the Wesleyan Methodist Conference in Britain. This raised sharp pastoral and disciplinary problems for the Wesleyans. Opposition to him reached a peak at the Conference in 1846 when, by a majority vote, it was resolved that he should no longer be allowed to use Wesleyan Methodist premises. In 1847, after a period of uncertainty, he returned to America. As Richard Carwardine has pointed out, the sides taken over the Caughey affair corresponded closely with those adopted in the split which, as already observed, was shortly to occur over wider issues in Wesleyan Methodism. 'Far from bringing peace and cohesion' to the unsettled ranks within Wesleyanism, Caughey 'brought aggravation, divisiveness, and an unsettling passion for souls'.[32] This episode, and to a less extent other developments including Charles Finney's writings and visit to Britain from 1849 to 1851, form part of the background against which Arthur's view of, and commitment to, revival has to be examined.

In *The Tongue of Fire* Arthur argued that the early church, at and after Pentecost, witnessed conversions on a massive scale, which was a clear sign of the activity of God and enabled whole generations of people to escape judgment. The word of God spread rapidly, he insisted. It did not advance 'with the moderation dear to small and proper men'.[33] Believing in the same Holy Spirit, Arthur therefore looked for revival with confidence:

> I expect to see cities swept from end to end, their manners elevated, their commerce purified, their politics Christianized, their criminal population reformed, their poor made to feel that they dwell amongst brethren, – righteousness in the streets, peace in the homes.[34]

Developments in the previous hundred years also encouraged Arthur to believe that theirs was 'pre-eminently the age of opportunity'.[35] These included improvements in travel and communication; the re-awakening of evangelical religion in Europe and America; greater openness to Christian influences in such places as Africa, China and some Muslim countries; and an increase in the number of evangelical ministers and agencies which potentially were instruments for the conversion of others. Ministers should not be locked into activities within the church, however important, but should be released to be engaged more in evangelism. He, however, read the signs of the times over-optimistically, declaring that every system of religion not calling itself Christian was decaying.

At the same time Arthur was also conscious of obstacles to revival. Even in England, he observed, public and private morality was at a low ebb. In the wider world superstition, oppression and corruption were rampant, and the church had scarcely begun to explore the world, let alone to occupy it with and for Christ. The conversion of the world would only be possible if people raised their sights, took God's promises seriously and depended more on his power. Aim at few conversions, and only few will be won. Aim at many, and the nineteenth century could witness a greater revival than ever before. Achievements already made suggested that 'the entire conversion of England and America' within fifty years would not be as great a work, with present resources, as had been accomplished in the last century.[36]

Arthur took a keen interest in the revival in Ulster in 1859, reading accounts of it in London and observing it at first hand on visits to Northern Ireland. His eight 'penny' pamphlets on aspects of revival reiterated some of the points already made in *The Tongue of Fire*, and took his thinking further. Expressing the hope that there might be a general rather than just a local revival, he defined a 'great revival' as 'a pervasive, national quickening' influencing every parish and touching society as a whole.[37] Such a movement would advance the cause of vital religion in ways similar to that achieved in the previous three centuries through the Reformation, the Puritan movement and the Evangelical Revival. The need was self-evident in view of widespread irreligion and apathy. The motivation was three-fold, namely the glory of God, the salvation of one's own people and the salvation of others.

Resistance to revival within the church came from the comfortable and the complacent. 'The dead members of a dead Church are . . . uneasy at any sign of a shaking among the dry bones,' he wrote. They experienced 'a fear of the return of life'.[38] Unbelief in the church was an obstacle that had to be removed. 'With faith, simple, firm, fast-holding faith', he affirmed, all such opposition could be overcome.[39] Although there would be opposition from society at large, there was also within every human heart a conscience to which an evangelical appeal could be addressed:

> Every man has a conscience; and it is on our side. It may be blinded, hushed, drugged, stupified; but it is not dead . . . Sin is strong in the fallen heart; but the Cross is strong in the universal conscience.[40]

In contrast to the position taken by some Calvinists, Arthur maintained that Christ had died for all and was able to save all:

> The whole tenor of the New Testament and the Old is, that the ruin of a soul is against the will of God . . . "All", "every man", the "world", the "whole world", are the terms employed, without any hint once again that a limit should be placed on their signification . . . This is the firm and broad foundation of our faith for national, wide-spread, universal revivals of religion, for the regeneration of our country, for the conversion of the world. We seek not a few; we seek as many as Jesus bought – all.[41]

In the voice of Christ's 'ever-speaking blood', wrote Arthur, could be heard 'the whole Godhead uttering immeasurable love, and beseeching us to be reconciled to God'.[42] There could be no surer grounds for revival.

On the fruits of revival, Arthur drew on what he had observed or been told in Ulster. There, it was claimed, every aspect of the church's life had been increased or enlivened, for example its preaching, praying, fellowship and outreach. There was evidence too of moral 'miracles' and of 'the elevating power' in society,[43] with religious bigotry reduced, poverty lessened and family life enhanced. The wiser use of money, and the spending of more time at home, were important elements in this. Conversions were therefore not only beneficial to the individuals concerned, Arthur claimed, but extended their influence to whole neighbourhoods.

As a result of the three previous major spiritual movements – the Reformation and the Puritan and Evangelical Revivals – separate denominations had been formed. There had been about them 'a terrible clang of polemical steel', Arthur noted. Perhaps in this instance, he hoped, there could be an absence of strife and instead a 'revival of union'.[44] Time was to reveal, however, that this dream would not be fulfilled. Sharp controversies arose in Ulster and elsewhere, although undoubtedly good was also done.

In praying and preparing for revival, according to Arthur, it was important to hold oneself in readiness as an instrument of God's purpose, affirming biblical truths and waiting expectantly upon God. Sensitive to earlier criticisms, he insisted that attempts to manufacture a revival by human contrivance should be avoided:

> Let us form no plans, set our eye on no particular Preacher, and shun everything like an effort to get up a revival . . . Let our whole plan be Union, Prayer, and Faith.[45]

In particular those preachers who possessed a reputation as 'revivalists', should be careful not to intrude or impose themselves. Though firmly committed to revival, therefore, Arthur favoured only a spontaneous movement.

He was particularly sensitive to criticisms of revival, including charges of fanaticism and 'extravagances',[46] and claimed that in Ulster he saw little evidence of emotional outbursts. On the contrary he noted that in Coleraine 'it was calm, very calm – almost dull'.[47] After a mammoth rally in Belfast's Botanical Gardens he commented that he had heard 'more vociferation &

rant' in a prayer meeting in Leeds than in all the events he had attended in Ulster.[48] None the less he admitted that there had been instances of 'extraordinary agitation of mind and body', starting in Ahoghill and spreading elsewhere. There had been similar developments in revivals in other parts of the world, including England, Sweden and America. These phenomena were not different, he argued, from descriptions in the Bible when, for example, the repentant David felt that his bones 'waxed old, through my roaring all the day long'.[49] What was essential, Arthur insisted, was that such emotion should not be artificially contrived. Although firmly of the view that God punished sin and that people perished without Christ, he also believed that people's emotions should not be manipulated. The crucial test in assessing the genuineness of emotional outbursts was whether they led to transformed lives.

It will come as no surprise that Arthur was taken to task over his coverage of the revival in Ulster. A fellow Methodist accused him of having 'truckled to Presbyterian prejudices' in that in his writings Arthur had drawn largely on Presbyterian sources. Yet, his critic alleged, extreme forms of Calvinism persisted in Ulster which were antagonistic to the revival, and Arthur's own tract *Did Christ die for All?* had come under fire in Presbyterian circles. Perhaps, it was suggested, he was now bidding to boost sales of his publications among Presbyterians.[50]

Isaac Nelson, a Presbyterian minister and nationalist who later entered parliament as a Parnellite, saw little good in the revival. He rejected comparison with earlier outpourings of the Holy Spirit and, incidentally, made it clear that such comparisons did not originate with Arthur:

> We must indignantly denounce every attempt to fasten the name Revival on the transaction recorded in the second chapter of the Acts of the Apostles ... Tell the Reformers of swooning, prostration, convulsions, and visions, as concomitants, much less signs, of the Spirit's work in the soul, and they would have sternly pointed to Holy Scripture, as a corrective of all such vagaries. No epileptic brain-stricken Revivalists were the high-minded Puritans.[51]

Nelson also rejected, as misinterpretations of scripture, the alleged principles on which revivalist views were said to be based, poured scorn on the 'talkative youths'[52] who emerged as spokesmen during the revival, and argued that party spirit had increased rather than lessened. Certainly the claim that anti-Catholicism was significantly reduced as a result of the revival cannot be substantiated except anecdotally and in isolated instances. Violent sectarianism continued to be a feature of life nearly every year after 1859. For example, following a large rally in Belfast in 1862, there was a serious outbreak of inter-communal violence. After Orange celebrations in July 1863, hostile mobs engaged each other, and in 1864 Belfast experienced its most savage religio-political disturbances of the period, eleven lives being lost.[53]

Any disappointment Arthur may have felt, that the 1859 revival was not more widespread and sustained, did not diminish his commitment to the concept of revival. In his opening statement as President of the Wesleyan Conference in 1866, Arthur invited members to join him in two petitions, that God's love would be perfected in his heart and that God would 'save thousands of souls'.[54] In a presidential address the following year, at the anniversary of Wesleyan Home Missions, he affirmed his belief in the sovereignty of God and denied that a revival could be brought about as and when people wanted. At the same time he also declared his conviction that God's sovereignty would be exercised on behalf of revival in response to 'united, persevering, believing prayer'. They should therefore 'train their hearts' to look for 'a great work of God'.[55] Some will conclude that at this point he was presuming too much. As an incentive to positive thinking, he pointed out that the increase in Methodist membership in the ten years prior to 1865 was greater than in any other ten year period with the exception of 1806 to 1816, and that it was as large as the total number of members in the United Kingdom up to the death of John Wesley. He took up the theme of revival again at the laying of the foundation stone for the Theological Institute at Headingley, Leeds, in 1867. Replying to his own question, as to how the world could be converted, he maintained that it only could come about through the exercise of spiritual gifts and not through changes in forms or structures. 'Let us ask for the return of Pentecostal days', he urged.[56] Later, in another address, he pressed candidates for ordination to bring the people in their care first to salvation, then to 'full salvation'. In one year it was possible, he claimed, that they could see Methodist numbers doubled and the whole nation influenced.[57]

Lest his reference to 'the return of Pentecostal days' be misunderstood, he made it clear that what was required was not what today would be termed 'power ministries'. More important than speaking with tongues and healing miracles was the ability to prophesy in a wider sense than fore-telling, proclaiming God's word so as to challenge, exhort, edify and comfort (I Cor 14.1).[58] Arthur had taken this same line much earlier in *The Tongue of Fire*, when in discussing the effects of being filled with the Holy Spirit according to New Testament teaching, he placed the emphasis on inner moral and spiritual change rather than on miracles or tongues. Further, he argued, tongues indicated an ability to speak foreign languages, not unknown languages, to enable the gospel to be communicated at the commencement of a new age:

> Speaking unknown tongues was never heard of in the apostolic days. That *miracle* first occurred in London some years ago. On the day of Pentecost no man pretended to speak unknown tongues; but, just as if we in London suddenly began to speak German, French, Spanish, Russian, Turkish, and other foreign languages, so it was with them.[59]

Arthur is presumably recalling the events in London surrounding the colourful and controversial Edward Irving in the early 1830s, when some of the earliest modern instances of speaking in tongues occurred. Irving was minister of the Church of Scotland congregation in Hatton Garden at the time, but was forced to leave the church by the trustees. He helped to establish the Catholic Apostolic Church in which a mixture of adventism, tongues and elaborate liturgy emerged. Arthur's stance on these issues was consistent throughout his life. Addressing the second ecumenical Methodist Conference in 1891, he again insisted that Pentecostal power was most evident not in healings or tongues but in the increase of believers and in godly lives. 'When the sound of the rushing mighty wind had ceased, and the cloven tongues of flame had disappeared', he proclaimed, 'the three thousand men and women living new lives remained.'[60]

Arthur's vision for the church was of every member in the body of Christ becoming activated by the Holy Spirit. Writing of Pentecost, he pointed out that each person received the gift of the Holy Spirit directly. He had not, for instance, been given first to the twelve to be communicated to the seventy, and then passed on to others. Similarly, he argued, the work of the church was not to become the preserve of its ordained ministers. Every believer had a part to play, with none 'mere adherents'. All were to be 'living, speaking, burning agents' in the life of the church and its witness to the world:

> Who could think that the new religion was ever to come down to this? that speaking of its joys, its hopes, its pardon, its mercy for the wide world, was to be considered a professional work, for set solemnities alone, and not to be a daily joy . . . to ever-growing multitudes? . . . Cheerless is the work of that Christian Minister, who, at set times, raises his testimony in the ears of a people, all of whom make a practice of hiding it in their hearts.[61]

Spiritual gifts and offices varied greatly within the church, in degree, honour and authority, according as the Spirit distributed them. Those who possessed the less ought to respect those who had the greater; the greater should not attempt to dominate or extinguish the lesser. To limit the exercise of spiritual gifts to the ordained ministry, would be to depart from New Testament Christianity.

Arthur was in good standing with evangelicals in other churches, and played an important part in the counsels and activities of the Evangelical Alliance. He attended the inaugural meeting of the Alliance in 1846, at which he proposed a resolution expressing concern for the universal spread of Christ's kingdom.[62] An address he gave to the annual conference of the Alliance in 1850 was published and widely circulated. Its main thrust was the organization's role in bringing evangelicals together and in promoting church union.[63] Evangelical co-operation, church union and mission were inter-related themes on which he regularly spoke. 'Everything tending to the union of the church, tends to the enlightening of the world', he claimed.[64] Arthur was elected to the Alliance's Executive Council in 1854, and became an

Honorary Secretary in 1867. He continued to hold the latter position until 1900.

To Arthur the greatness of England was 'essentially a Protestant greatness', superior in every way to what could be achieved through Roman Catholicism.[65] Wherever the latter became dominant, he claimed, a nation's laws, education and morals were inferior. Its press was fettered, its people oppressed and its foreign enterprises unsuccessful. A passing remark in his lecture on the British Empire illustrates his belief in the moral superiority of evangelical Christianity. The Maltese were like the Italians, he observed, 'very devout and very immoral', adding that this was not an unusual combination in both Roman Catholic and heathen countries.[66] It was all the more important therefore that evangelicals upheld biblical truth, lived exemplary lives and engaged in Christ's mission.

4

Communicator

William Arthur was a skilled communicator, as preacher, public speaker and writer. The commemorative window to him in Wesley's Chapel, London, entitled 'The Sower', is a reminder of this.

Preacher and Speaker

Arthur's pulpit and platform ministry, greatly restricted by ill health after his early thirties, was most effective in the period following his return from India in 1841. His years in London as assistant to John Scott at Wesley's Chapel, and in association with the WMMS, were high points, when he was much in demand for chapel openings and anniversaries, public meetings and especially for overseas mission events. By the late 1840s, however, he was having difficulty with hoarseness, and in the early 1850s his voice lost its power and reliability.

Eloquent and with a choice command of language, Arthur was 'a superb Irish orator'.[1] He was not, however, a popular preacher in the accepted sense, avoiding humour, personal references and light anecdotes. 'A man who talks about himself has a fool for his subject', he said to an American audience in 1891.[2] The illustrations he used in public speaking reflected wide reading and reveal him as a gifted interpreter of life, ranging in content from every day incident to scientific observation. He handled large themes, not impersonally or academically but with passion, often conveying to his hearers a profound sense of God's presence and power. He was a strong believer in extempore preaching, preparing thoroughly, unconfined by a manuscript, and speaking from the heart in a way that left him open to God's prompting. At one period he confessed to being under pressure, with little opportunity to prepare beforehand, and confided 'I take texts & pour out a heap of reflexions (sic) & emotions, as they are given to me.'[3] Young preachers should be set on fire, he urged, being taught to avoid 'all fiddle faddle, finery & essayfying'. It was their solemn and urgent task to call people to God.[4] James Nicholls, the printer and author, heard Arthur preach regularly at Wesley's Chapel, and expressed the opinion that there was often more material in his introductions than in the whole of many sermons from others.[5] After hearing a sermon by Arthur on a passage in Revelation, Rigg declared that he had never heard it bettered.[6]

It was, however, as a spokesman on behalf of missions that Arthur excelled, defending them stoutly against misunderstanding and misrepresentation, and commending them warmly to the entire connexion. In his advocacy of missions he united information, conviction and passion in a rare and telling combination. When Arthur died in 1901, John Telford expressed the opinion that no other person had aroused such enthusiasm for missions.[7]

Arthur's writings and addresses discussed the theory and art of preaching. In an article on Jabez Bunting in the *London Quarterly Review* in 1859 he identified three kinds of speaking i.e. impromptu, extemporaneous and memoriter. The first he described in terms of conversation and reply in debate, when both the thoughts and their expression in words have to come on the spur of the moment. The second is exemplified in the speech of an advocate, statesman or preacher who has thoroughly mastered his subject and is able to express himself freely without having to recall particular words or phrases. The third is the speech of a boy or actor who has learnt his words in precise order, and can repeat them verbatim. Arthur summarized their uses:

> He who always speaks impromptu becomes vapid; he who generally speaks memoriter, stiff and stilted; he who generally speaks extemporaneously, not shrinking from impromptu when called by necessity, and using recitation occasionally as an exercise, will probably develop his powers as far as they are capable.[8]

Arthur saw in Bunting an example of the best kind of extempore speaker, a person in command of what he had to say as a result of thorough preparation, so that even impromptu comments contained 'nuggets of sense'.[9] His addresses took, as it were, the form of 'a well-twined electric cable, coiled in the mind', which could run off at ease, and along which the battery of his heart could transmit messages that seemed to come from the other world.[10]

Attention to the details of preparation was essential, including the structure and composition of addresses, pronunciation and a grasp of the subject. This would not ensure success, however. As Arthur wryly remarked, 'a good dinner badly cooked is spoiled, and so is a good discourse ill-delivered'.[11] These words take on special significance when it is recalled that for long periods ill health silenced him, and compelled him to sit under the pulpit ministry of others. He was in a better position than most to assess the efforts of fellow-preachers. A preacher had first to acquit himself simply as a speaker, and had therefore to learn how best to use his voice to effect, paying attention to such things as breathing, pitch and voice projection. These were areas in which preachers, to be effective, needed gifts, grace and training.

At the same time Arthur recognized that training could point preachers in the wrong direction. They needed to take care not to become mere 'mouthing elocutionists',[12] and should avoid aiming primarily at producing literary effect. Preachers should not seek to give intellectual pleasure instead of religious impressions, and nothing should be allowed to interfere with their reliance on God. This was the background to Arthur's criticism of the use of manuscripts by preachers. Whether actually at hand in the pulpit or stored in the memory, manuscripts distracted preachers from trust in God, he argued. Scripts might well promote intellectual gratification and literary style, but they also impeded the free flow of communication between God and preacher and between preacher and people. Spiritual blessing could still result, Arthur acknowledged, but:

> it is not scriptural preaching. It is not ministering after the mode of Pentecostal Christianity; it is a departure from scriptural precedent, an adoption of a lower order of public ministration, and a solemn declaration that security of utterance gained by natural supports, is preferred over a liability to be humiliated by trusting to the help of the Lord. It has its clear

advantages, and its clear losses. It secures a gain of elegance, at the cost of ease, – of finish, at the cost of freedom, – of precision, at that of power, – and of literary pleasure, at that of religious impressiveness.[13]

Not surprisingly this passage in *The Tongue of Fire* (1856), drew unfavourable comment. In an article in the *London Quarterly Review*, warmly appreciative of the book in general, it was conceded that there were 'many subordinate topics' connected with practical aspects of preaching on which Arthur had expressed a personal view-point with candour. These, the reviewer anticipated, would be 'found out in due time', adding that it was not the business of the paper to take sides. 'We must leave the troubler of our *memoriter* and manuscript preachers to fight his own battles with them', he wrote ominously.[14] The reviewer did, however, make some relevant points – that the use of a manuscript and memory could indeed aid, rather than hinder, trust in God; that historically some of the most powerful preaching had contravened Arthur's principles; that the apostles themselves had quoted the Old Testament prophets and Psalms at length from memory, when preaching; and that those taking a contrary position to Arthur on this point should not be excluded from the category of scriptural preachers.

The reviewer's instinct proved correct, and the following year another Wesleyan author, James Kendall, in a twenty-page pamphlet, took Arthur to task over the practical section of the book. He noted the faults of what he termed 'loose incoherent extemporizers',[15] and pressed that inexperienced preachers in particular would benefit from the use of notes and trained memory, and that other preachers should be left to do what they considered best for themselves without being subject to criticism. He also argued that there was no contradiction between aiming at literary effect and at religious effect, so long as the former was subordinate. Indeed the 'tacit condemnation of correct and well ordered speech, and indirect recommendation of rudeness and vulgarity' had done a lot of harm, and was distasteful to many, he claimed.[16] He added that providing intellectual stimulus and pleasure could lead to religious impressions. 'Fire', Kendall insisted, should not be identified in the main with extempore speech, certainly not with what could degenerate into 'mere noise and rant'.[17] Just as it could be kindled by the scriptures well read, it could result from a carefully prepared sermon delivered in the form in which it had been written. The special demands involved in occupying the same pulpit week by week, with the need for variety and freshness, had not been appreciated. If preaching from the apostles onwards had been in the extempore form, how could theological libraries have been stocked and devotional sermons passed on for the nourishment of many? Why, he asked, do good men who reason so well on other subjects, 'speak and write so loosely and inaccurately on *preaching*?' Clearly there was substance in these criticisms, and there is some indication that Arthur later softened his approach on these points.

So far as preaching style was concerned, Arthur encouraged each person to discover what suited him best. Comparison of different styles was like asking whether the rifle, carbine, or cannon was the best weapon. Each was best it its own place. What really mattered was that a person used whichever was 'right' for him, that he charged it well, and that he saw it was in a condition to strike fire. Style was secondary, spiritual power primary, he argued.[18] People varied enormously from such points of view as talent, education and intellectual ability, but what was most required was for each preacher to be an instrument of God's power. He must himself enjoy a close relationship with God, and hold God's fire within his heart 'as a Leyden jar will hold the invisible electricity'.[19] He must then have a conductor to communicate the fire to his hearers. 'There is but one conductor', declared Arthur, 'and that is the word of Life.' The way for preachers and churches to receive power was through prayer, 'prayer earnest, prayer united, and prayer persevering'.[20]

Arthur held clear views about the purpose of preaching. It was not so that the preacher could acquit himself well, or to enable him to please or to entertain an audience. It was rather 'to produce instant and lasting religious impressions' which could take various forms according to people's stages of development and needs.[21] At all times there should be a concern to bring people to a saving faith in Jesus Christ. The power to be coveted by the preacher, and available as God's gift, is 'converting power'.[22] Arthur himself manifested a concern for souls as a teenager in the west of Ireland, while at the Theological Institution at Hoxton, as a missionary in India and at each point thereafter. Even as an old man addressing ministerial students in America, this was his main thrust. 'You are here in a lost world', he declared, 'and God has saved you that you may be part of His instrumentality in saving the rest of the world.' Referring to the one thing worth aiming at, he went on:

> The spirit in which that aim is to be pursued is indicated in the word of Paul: 'My little children, of whom I travail in birth again until Christ be formed in you.' The father-spirit, the parent-spirit, that will go through any agony that will not be content to leave the child unsaved, and that knows that the process of saving is the formation of Christ in the heart! Have you ever wrestled in secret for a soul? ... A man, when he is in that state of mind, is not in a condition ... to be much impressed by the poets and the *litterateurs* and magazine writers and infidel writers of the day.[23]

As preachers of the gospel they had a part to play in bringing civilization to people, in educating them, and in enabling them to become good citizens, but none of these activities or others related to them should have first call on their talent or effort. They had to aim higher, and if they hit the mark they would register achievements at lower levels too. If they did good to a man's soul, they would benefit him in every way – his principles, intellect, emotions and habits – and would also influence his family and neighbourhood for good.

When it came to the content of sermons, Arthur made demands on the mental powers of his listeners by preaching on great doctrinal themes. His description of Jabez Bunting was true of himself, that he was 'no perfunctory lecturer' discussing subjects of substance and interest for a time and then setting them aside. He was an ambassador with a message to proclaim and a people to win.[24] Arthur proclaimed the central evangelical truths, but found, as he had learnt in India, that key words of the faith such as atonement, justification, regeneration and resurrection could be unintelligible to listeners. They could not be abandoned, however. The need therefore was to communicate the concepts rather than the terms, by interpreting, illustrating, and applying them.[25]

It has been said that in much contemporary theology the wrath of God is 'an industriously evaded doctrine'.[26] Arthur noted a tendency in this direction in his day, but firmly believed that the note of judgment should not be muffled. In Britain as much as in India the preacher must not fear to speak of God's anger against sin. In speaking on this theme in Exeter Hall, London, in 1856 he based his address on Psalm 7.11, 'God judgeth the righteous, and God is angry with the wicked every day.' Biblical religion, he declared – of the New as of the Old Testament – is a religion that 'will give sin no quarter, that everywhere meets it sternly, and everywhere denounces it without compromise'. 'There is an anger of benevolence,' he argued.[27] At the human level it is kindled when wrong is done, and when those we love take the path to their own undoing. God's anger is of this kind. Terrible as it is, its absence would be more terrible. God's anger is an inevitable result of his purity, is an expression of his justice, and is a measure of the loving regard he has for us. It is a forbearing anger, so that though judgment is prepared, it is not yet executed. A mediator is provided. Those who repent and trust in him find that God's anger, which is forgiving as well as forbearing, is turned away.[28]

Arthur's topics in the addresses he gave from public platforms, several of them delivered in London before the Young Men's Christian Association, were wide-ranging. In some he faced issues of the day. For example, from the mid- to late 1840s he spoke on 'ragged schools' for destitute children, Islam, the British Empire, India and the French Revolution. At other times he addressed an audience in Belfast on Christian giving, with an Anglican bishop in the chair; and spoke to people in Folkestone on riots in Jamaica and the coverage they were given in the British press. The addresses, though of considerable length and containing detailed information, were prepared and delivered without notes, and were subsequently published. One featured a favourable, if somewhat romanticized, view of the extension of British influence through-out the world. Others reflected social and political conservatism, with an acceptance of capitalism and a concern that people become self-reliant. Other points included a belief in the superiority of Christianity over other faiths, religion as a source of moderation and as a means of social control, a need for Christianity to be expressed in ways relevant to life, and a rejection of the tenets of Roman Catholicism and a suspicion of its influence in society.

James Rigg has indicated how Arthur prepared lectures and sermons by 'premeditation', without a sentence being written in preparation or to aid delivery.[29] This was a skill Arthur was forced to acquire especially in the months following his return to England from India, when, under medical care, he had to refrain as far as possible from reading and writing. Even when his condition improved to the extent that, with coloured glasses, he could read good print by daylight, he still attempted to prepare as far as possible by mental processes without the use of his eyes. Rigg described how Arthur prepared and delivered the famous lecture on the British Empire:

> The delivery of that lecture occupied, perhaps, two hours. It was delivered without note from first to last; it was prepared without a sentence having been written, by the wonderful power of premeditation which Mr Arthur possessed. That power . . . embraced, of course, the general ideas underlying the lecture, and the order in which they were to be explained, including the statistics, and especially the lessons to be derived from the survey. But, besides this general power of memory apart from writing, Mr Arthur was able so exactly to fix special passages in his mind by close premeditation that the language of such passages could be delivered in exact correspondence with his mental forecast.[30]

He had accordingly no manuscript of the lecture which he had delivered. Provision had therefore been made for the best possible shorthand report of the address to be made. This was sent to him and corrected for publication. Possessing such an exceptional memory was an undoubted asset, especially since the use of his eyes was restricted. By his own definition, however, he was an 'extemporaneous' rather than a 'memoriter' preacher.

In Arthur's view the role of the preacher was decisive in communicating God's word. Preachers varied enormously in ability, but they must all possess sufficient. The suggestion by some people that there would be benefit in having 'weak instruments in the ministry' was 'without a tittle of scriptural foundation'. True, to the wise of this world the cross in itself is 'foolishness', but 'Christ never sends fools to be its heralds'.[31] Similarly the institution of preaching, as a means of regeneration, is in itself 'foolishness', but 'none of the preachers sent of God were simpletons'. Those without gifts to teach or preach should find out what they are suited for and pursue that line. They should not 'pule about the Lord delighting to use foolish instruments'. Those called by God to preach may lack the knowledge and talent to talk on secular subjects, but they are people of sense, they possess speaking ability and, above all, they have the spiritual power to address people's hearts and 'to act upon the conscience'.[32] On offering for the ministry they were initially tested on the basis of their gifts, awareness of a call and their knowledge of God at work within their own lives. Those requirements were constants. A minister could not be held responsible for 'success', but he was responsible for continuing to trust in God and for remaining an instrument of God's Spirit. These ensured a proper sense of seriousness and urgency in ministry, so that a preacher would not be content to 'deal out dainties from the pulpit' or to 'spin fine paragraphs for the winding-sheet or (dying) souls' committed to their care.[33] In the end the word preached would be effective, not primarily because of the talents of preachers, but because it was the *word of God*. Preachers were to be channels of God's word.

Writer

Arthur's literary output was prodigious by any standard. He wrote on a wide range of topics over a period of half a century. The first of his published volumes appeared in 1847, the last forty years later. In addition he published a large number of lectures, pamphlets, letters and articles. The lecture on the British Empire appeared in 1845. His last article, in 1899, was an attempt to anticipate the twentieth century from a missionary perspective. Periods of rest and travel, necessitated by recurring bouts of ill health, undoubtedly facilitated the gathering of material and the making of important contacts, but poor sight and prolonged weakness were inhibiting factors.

Arthur's writings reflected wide interests and deep concerns. As his ability to speak in public lessened, his writings became more important since he had much to communicate. Many of the contents of the writings are indicated in these pages, with quotations to illustrate the clarity of Arthur's thinking and the forcefulness of his views. Much that he wrote reveals an over-all missionary concern, with two publications focussing directly on this theme, *A Mission to the Mysore* (1847) and *Women's Work in India* (1883).

His main writings on Roman Catholicism extended over a quarter of a century. Articles included 'Ultramontanism' (1853), 'The Pope's Encyclical' (1865), and 'The Vatican and the Kremlin' (1866). His major opus in this field was *The Pope, the Kings, and the People* (1877), but the earlier *Italy in Transition* (1860), though primarily providing a human perspective on political developments in Italy, also contained a lot of material on Roman Catholicism. Letters to the press reflected his concern over matters of public interest, prominent among them being contributions to the *Daily News* on education and to *The Times* on Home Rule proposals for Ireland. His pamphlet *Shall the Loyal be Deserted and the Disloyal set over Them?* (1886), also on Home Rule, was widely read. Among writings on church and theological matters, were an article 'Methodism and the Established Church' (1856), eight 'penny' pamphlets on revival in the late 1850s, and two other pamphlets, *Ought Not the Two Methodist Bodies in Ireland to Become One?* (1869) and *Divinity of our Lord in Relation to His Work of Atonement* (1885). Also in this category was *The Tongue of Fire* (1856), which continued to be read into this century. A centenary edition was published in 1956. It is marked by a passionate concern for the renewal of the church, especially of the ministry, while at the same time playing down miraculous phenomena. Here, as in other writings, Arthur avoided extreme positions. For example, in a discussion on 'set' prayers and 'free' prayer, he insisted on the value of both:

> He who will never use a form in public prayer, casts away the wisdom of the past. He who will use only forms, casts away the hope of utterance to be given by the Spirit at present, and even shuts up the future in the stiff hand of the past . . . To object to all forms is narrowness. To doom a

Christian temple to be a place wherein a simple and impromptu cry may never arise to heaven, is superstition.[34]

Nor did Arthur plead for some unvarying method of receiving or displaying the Holy Spirit's power.

A long-term interest in philosophy culminated in several publications in the 1880s, with *On the Difference between Physical and Moral Law* (1883), *Religion without God* and *God without Religion* (1885 – 1888), and *On Time and Space, Two Witnesses for a Creator* (1887). *The Successful Merchant* (1852), a biography of Samuel Budgett, a Bristol businessman, was valued at the time as an attempt to apply Christian principles to business practice, but it has also been criticized as a eulogy of capitalism. A highly critical review appeared in the *Wesleyan Times*, accusing Arthur of wordiness, inaccuracy and literary self-indulgence. The reviewer also claimed that Samuel Budgett, whom Arthur had not known personally, was an unsuitable subject for such a study, describing him as 'a Sabbath-breaking, mammon-loving tradesman'. Arthur, it was argued, would have served his reading public better had he chosen Samuel's half-brother, Henry, as his subject.[35] In assessing these comments, account has to be taken of the bitter divisions within Methodism at that time. The *Wesleyan Times* was the newspaper of a reform element, and attacks on Wesleyan 'establishment' figures, such as Arthur had become, were commonly featured in its pages. It is therefore impressive that only four years later the same paper carried a highly appreciative review of *The Tongue of Fire*.[36] This indicated both a lessening of hostilities and Arthur's ability to make friends in different 'camps'. His other biography, *The Life of Gideon Ouseley* (1876), reflects the florid style found in some Victorian writing, but it remains a useful introduction to a colourful and significant Irish evangelist. Invitations to write further biographies were declined.[37]

Recurring features in Arthur's writing include his descriptive and analytical powers, a facility for producing memorable phrases and a fondness for 'purple passages'. He made frequent use of analogy, often of a scientific nature:

When a lecturer on electricity wants to show an example of a human body surcharged with his fire, he places a person on a stool with glass legs. The glass serves to isolate him from the earth, because it will not conduct the fire, – the electric fluid: were it not for this, however much might be poured into his frame, it would be carried away by the earth; but, when thus isolated from it, he retains all that enters him. You see no fire, you hear no fire; but you are told that it is pouring into him. Presently you are challenged to the proof, – asked to come near, and hold your hand close to his person: when you do so, a spark of fire shoots out towards you. If thou, then, wouldst have thy soul surcharged with the fire of God, so that those who come nigh to thee shall feel some mysterious influence proceeding out from thee, thou must draw nigh to the source of that fire, to the throne of God . . . and shut thyself out from the world, – that cold world, which so swiftly steals our fire away.[38]

One writer has recently suggested that what he described as Arthur's 'urbane and genteel phraseology' in *The Tongue of Fire* may have diminished his impact.[39] The description of Arthur's style is apt, at least by today's standards. Yet the initial impact of the message of *The Tongue of Fire*, either proclaimed as an address or presented in book form, was enormous. Also those who read Arthur's philosophical writings are impressed by the clarity and well-defined nature of much that he wrote. This is in marked contrast to the language used by many philosophers of that period and since.

T.B. Stephenson queried whether Arthur was '*the* most prolific Methodist writer' since John Wesley.[40] It is difficult to see by what criteria this could be judged. If by quantity alone it would seem unlikely, even though he published much. Even when due allowance has been made for the fact that some of Arthur's writing was ephemeral, and that other parts have become dated, the abiding impression is of its range and quality.

5

Missionary

Mission was William Arthur's abiding passion. His first book focussed on the theme,[1] and his last article, written more than fifty years later, anticipated the twentieth century from the point of view of mission.[2] Throughout his active ministry Arthur was linked in some way with the Wesleyan Methodist Missionary Society (WMMS). Indeed it could be argued that mission was the standpoint from which he viewed all other matters such as education, inter-church relations, Roman Catholicism, the role of Britain in the world and Home Rule in Ireland. His abiding concern was for whatever would best promote evangelical Christianity and the values associated with it. Most of the material in this book is therefore relevant to Arthur's understanding of, and involvement in, mission.

Although sharply critical of the abuses of colonialism, for example in Tasmania,[3] Arthur was a convinced colonialist. He saw the hand of God, not mere commercial or political self-interest, in the extension of British influence and control in the world. The possession of colonies, he argued, carried with it humanitarian obligations and opened the door to immense spiritual opportunity. In addressing the Anniversary Meeting of the WMMS in 1848, he declared:

> We may look at our colonies as a great means for the extension of our national grandeur. But take another view. Take their geographical position, and they present a most astonishing opening, furnished by the providence of God, to bring to bear upon every portion of the human race the energies of the Anglo-Saxon character, and the truths of the Christian faith.[4]

This continued to be his position throughout his life. In 1886, when he feared that Gladstone's Home Rule proposals for Ireland threatened the integrity of the British Empire, he recorded his conviction and hope:

> My faith in the mission of the British Empire was strong in youth ... My faith was still stronger when, in 1853, writing in the *London Quarterly*, I proposed its federation. Now, after comparison of many lands and many systems, it is stronger than ever. The Empire is not going to be wrecked. There is a blessing in it; and many of those who were ready to perish call it blessed ... I have heard the slave ransomed and the slave in bonds bless it ... The British have done a great thing. I have heard colonists of other nations say over and over again that if England had their country it would advance far faster ... It is not going to be destroyed.[5]

Ireland, Arthur believed, had been placed under Britain's protection by God. Faith as much as politics was therefore involved in resisting Home Rule and upholding the Empire. Opposition to the growth of Roman Catholic influence anywhere in the world was also an element in his world-view, since Romanism was seen as a rival, alien and illiberal force in the world. Arthur's interest in world affairs, as expressed for example in his informed writings about America, Italy, France and Russia, was not merely academic or secular. It also should be seen in the light of his belief in the international role of Britain and his concern for the spread of true Christian influences, as he understood them.

The impact of Arthur on Gubbi, Mysore, from 1839 to 1841 has been generously exaggerated. The mission was in its infancy when he joined it, and continued to limp along after his departure, being abandoned for a time in the 1850s. The influence of India upon Arthur, however, cannot be exaggerated. He, like many others, was changed for life by his Indian experience. It would also be difficult to over-emphasize the role of Arthur in Methodism's missionary outreach in the second half of the nineteenth century. His written and spoken advocacy of missions, so long as he had voice and energy, fired the imagination of countless people. His grasp of international and mission-related issues, acquired during two prolonged spells as a WMMS Secretary, coupled with firm convictions and deep insights, ensured that his mind would be sought and respected in church courts.

In *The Irish in World Methodism 1760–1900* attention has been drawn to several features of Arthur's missionary contribution.[6] On the primary and definitive nature of God's mission, he stressed the vital role of the Holy Spirit. God had spoken and acted decisively at Pentecost for the benefit of all peoples, letting loose a force which claimed all humanity. Without this power Christianity would become a human agency for social improvement, blessed with superhuman doctrines but destitute of superhuman power. In Jesus, Arthur argued, God's mission had been both defined and expressed. Other points of his teaching included the creative interplay between home and overseas missions, the need for social as well as personal renewal, the impotence of idolatry in contrast to the saving efficacy of Christ, the importance of Bible translation and distribution, and the need for missionaries to become skilled in the use of vernacular languages.

Although Arthur was an ardent supporter of the British Empire, it is impressive that he urged his fellow Britons not to assume that they held centre-stage in the world's affairs. A totally different world-view was required, he urged. Arthur was a committed European, in the non-political sense. He had lived in France, and had travelled in other countries, chiefly Germany and Italy, becoming familiar with their languages and literature. There had been a period, he acknowledged, when 'it seemed as if a man could hardly be a good Englishman unless he hated the French', and the French held similar views of the English. Times had now changed, when very different attitudes were required. The progress of civilization and new insights into the teaching of the Bible were factors in this:

> You will find in semi-civilised countries – and it is not so long ago since it was the case in parts of our islands, – that a man belonging to one clan or tribe, or faction, would think he hardly deserved the name if he did not count himself the standing enemy of every man that bore the other name. You love your own family, and therefore you are to stand in the way of another. That is Satan's perversion, but the religion of the Bible is this, – You love your own families, therefore

you are to consider the families of others; you love your own children, therefore you are to feel that your neighbour's children have the same rights as yours. And so it is to be with nations.[7]

Europeans, he argued, had to widen their thinking still further:

Far more than half the world never heard Napoleon's name . . . far more than half the world could not tell you whether Europe is one country or many. We are not a quarter of the world's population . . . From the soil of Asia man was formed, in Asia he had his Eden . . . in Asia he spent his early years, in Asia he has always had his chief dwelling, and on Asia dropped the blood that bought his ransom . . . If any section of the earth might call itself the world, Asia would be the world.[8]

Within Asia, he believed that India held the key to mission strategy. Win India for Christ, and victory would follow on other fronts, he claimed.

Arthur also insisted that all shared a common humanity. Any tendency towards racism, as had emerged in the British press after an uprising of black people in Jamaica, was stoutly resisted by Arthur. Black people had simply reacted to unjust conditions in much the same way as people of other races had done before them.[9] On aborigines in Australia, Arthur affirmed their essential humanity in contrast to those who regarded them as 'monkeys'. Drawing attention to their good qualities, he noted their acuteness of intellect, adaptability and gift for acquiring other languages. Their response to missionaries amply demonstrated 'their right to a place in the human family'.[10] This conviction of a shared humanity accounts for Arthur's abhorrence of slavery and, at another level, of the palanquin as a means of transport in India. The palanquin was 'unsocial', degrading to those used as mere beasts of burden.[11] This line of thought became a powerful element in the advocacy of mission:

Feel, oh feel, when you pray, that one-half of your brethren never heard of your Redeemer! Bone are they of your bone, flesh of your flesh, conflicting, sighing, bending to the grave like you; but crown for their conflicts, comforter in their sighs, hope in their grave, they see none.[12]

Hinduism ran counter to Christianity at this point, since caste essentially severed 'the cord of brotherhood'.[13] To a Hindu the idea that an outcaste sprang from the same stock as the rest of mankind was wholly unacceptable:

> Servitude is honour; slavery, brotherhood . . . compared with the fathomless degradation into which the poor out-caste is plunged. Father, mother, children, down they are sunk; all trample on them, all abuse, all revile, all execrate, all shun . . . By this horrid proscription, millions of human beings are being held in a state of anomalous slavery. No one claims their person – it is too vile; but, with limbs unchained, the man is denied every right of citizenship; he and his unborn children, and his children's children, are doomed to ignorance, exclusion, and contempt. He is an exile from the human family, cut off, and cut off for ever, from affection and improvement . . . The earth rejects him – he may not own a single rood; the water rejects him – his defiled vessel, or more defiled person, would pollute a whole well . . . Law rejects him – who is he that he should complain? Religion rejects him . . . Charity herself rejects him.[14]

Given the all-pervading influence of caste, Arthur held that change should only be introduced gradually since the re-education of a whole people was involved. As with West Indian slavery, the chain of eastern bondage should be 'gently melted' rather than 'rent' by force, to avoid the utter breakdown of society.[15]

In a similar way the low status of women was highlighted by Arthur, with Hinduism and Islam both coming in for criticism on account of their denial, in different ways, of education and other 'privileges' to women. Righteous indignation rather than respectful moderation should be the response in this connection:

> We should confront, with a wrath that could neither be appeased nor mitigated, the system that parts humanity into two different natures; that makes the sister her brother's inferior, the wife her husband's slave; that shuts up myriads

of intellects from all culture; that dooms families to despotism.[16]

Among women, young Hindu widows were to be pitied most, being subject to scorn, harsh treatment and social ostracism. The uninformed, romanticized 'Western' view of beautiful be-jewelled Asian women living in splendour in their separate apartments or Zenanas, was also held up to ridicule by Arthur, who presented a contrasting picture of squalor and of emotional and material deprivation. The heartfelt cry of an un-named Indian woman was given prominence by Arthur in his *Women's Work in India*:

> O Lord, hear my prayer! No one has turned an eye on the oppression that we poor women suffer, though with weeping, and crying, and desire, we have turned to all sides hoping that some would save us. No one has lifted up his eyelids to look upon us or inquire into our case ... We are like the dry husks of the sugar-cane when the sweet juice has been extracted. All-knowing God, hear our prayer, forgive our sins, and give us power of escape, that we may see something of Thy world ... From Thy throne of judgment justice flows, but it does not reach to us ... Criminals confined in the jails are happier than we for they know something of Thy world ... We see only the four walls of the house. Shall we call them the world or India? ... Dost Thou care only for men? Hast Thou no thought for us women? ... Create in the hearts of men some sympathy, that our lives may no longer be passed in vain longing, and that, saved by Thy mercy, we may taste something of the joys of life.[17]

Work by women missionaries was therefore of the utmost importance, in Arthur's view, given that they had access to people and places beyond the reach of men.

With regard to other faiths, Arthur believed that at an early period in history all had shared 'the true religion'. From Noah onwards, he claimed, 'all the various branches of the human family were instructed in the true religion'.[18] Apart from saying that this original and common form of religion included belief in an almighty, all-creating God, he did not, however, proceed to specify its tenets.

Arthur's view of Hinduism was overwhelmingly negative. As noted in *The Irish in World Methodism 1760–1900*, his main objection was that it failed to meet the deepest moral and spiritual needs of people.[19] For example, it clouded vital issues including the nature of the divine being, and it held an undeveloped view of sin. It failed to provide pardon and peace, despite all its emphasis on meditation, penance, ablutions and the repetition of mantras; and it offered no effective dynamic for holy living. He was particularly scornful of idolatry, stressing its impotence in every sphere apart from its capacity to corrupt. All of this led Arthur to present Christ uncompromisingly. He alone could fill the spiritual vacuum in people's hearts, opening up new life for them here and now without recourse to the necessity of re-births. This was the main thrust of Arthur's approach to Hinduism.

On closer investigation, however, some slightly more positive elements appear in Arthur's writings. At times he admitted to finding traces of earlier, less corrupt forms of Hinduism, which he interpreted as lingering evidence of the earlier 'true religion'. This had not been totally obliterated by later developments such as Brahmanism and idolatry. For example, although he felt the idea of God in the Shastras was 'lamentably entangled and obscure', what he called 'the primeval doctrine of the divine unity' had not been obliterated completely.[20] Similarly in discussing some passages in the Puranas he acknowledged that they reflected 'true ideas of God', including some awareness of 'the divine glory'.[21] Elsewhere, in a quotation about meditation on 'the supreme Being', he detected 'a ray of earlier light flitting among the shades that had fallen so thickly'.[22] None of this adds up to more than a few flickering lights in what to him was the otherwise unrelieved darkness of Hinduism. In Arthur's view, that light was insufficient to enable Hindus to become new and holy persons. Only the grace of God in Jesus Christ could assuredly effect that transformation.

On Islam, Arthur acknowledged that it was 'far from being godless or a negation of all religion'.[23] He welcomed, for example, its strong opposition to idolatry, and admitted that it had a part to play in changing society for the better. Its influence in this regard, however, was much less than was possible through Christianity. Recognizing its superiority over paganism, Arthur none the less believed that Islam too was inadequate at crucial points, being more 'a Christian heresy of the most fatal kind' than a genuinely original faith. The Koran, for example, recognized Jesus' divine mission, but denied his divine nature. Islam, he wrote:

> leaves man without any gospel of redemption, without any atonement before God, and without any clear account of the way whereby the sinful obtain grace. It also dooms private life to the miseries of polygamy, and leaves woman in a position of contempt. Nations it curses with a code of blood, which wields the conscience by the sword. In the character of its author we have a forcible contrast with the stainless purity of our blessed Redeemer.[24]

Arthur's reference to Islam's violation of people's consciences through the use of undue force is in line with his consistent emphasis that in Christian evangelism there should be no resort to material incentives or governmental pressures. An isolated statement by him on one occasion appears to be at odds with this stance, however, and is therefore puzzling and disturbing:

> I do seriously and joyfully believe that the rapid conquest gained over India by British arms, is the preparation and will prove the type of the conquest to be gained over it by the glorious gospel.[25]

'Type' here cannot refer to a total triumph in the religious sphere by similarly coercive methods. Such would be entirely out of character with Arthur's approach elsewhere. The reference, there-fore, must be to a swift spiritual conquest, without coercion, soon after the military conquest.

Given Arthur's largely negative understanding of other faiths, what did he feel a missionary could appeal to in his work of evangelism? If other faiths were not significant spiritual allies, could effective contact be established in some other way? His observation, already noted, that in every heart there is a conscience to which an appeal can be made, is relevant even though Arthur's use of it was with reference to England.[26] Although sin exercised a dominant influence in the unredeemed life, 'the Cross' was also 'strong in the universal conscience'. Arthur presumably thought of conscience as an indication of man's creation in the image of God. Other people, however, will take support from this reference to the cross, and from a further statement by Arthur, for their view that the existence of a universal conscience points in some sense to the presence and influence of Christ in every human heart:

> Hindus have not the well-taught tender conscience of a Christian; but they have that light from God in Christ which enables them . . . to discern in good a beauty, and in evil a stain, which makes the choice of the latter defiling.[27]

Reference to the 'light from God in Christ', and to the cross of Christ in relation to the universal conscience, does arguably modify Arthur's predominantly negative approach to Hinduism, even if this was not his intention.

Arthur believed firmly in universal atonement, that Christ had died for all and could save all, and in the missionary responsibility of all Christians. The Holy Spirit was God's gift at Pentecost to the whole church, to enable it to fulfil its role in this connection. The Spirit had been given to each Christian directly. Mission was not solely, or even initially, a task only for 'professionals'. All believers were to be engaged in sharing God's word with the world. Within this general commissioning of all Christians, individuals received particular callings.

Arthur's identification with the poor and the oppressed, together with his conviction that Christ alone could transform life, gave a sharp edge to his missionary commitment. It accounts too for his high view of missionary vocation. Considerations such as social acceptability, earning capacity and authority over others should not weigh heavily with Christians in the choice of career. Much more important was the privilege and the obligation of sharing Christ with others. What, he wondered, would be the ultimate destiny of 'money-clutching Christians'[28] who, knowing the spiritual plight of millions, preferred to lay up earthly treasures for themselves rather than to make others eternally rich? Parents were sometimes guilty of misdirecting their children in this matter:

> Those parents who consign their sons, who have the heart for a higher calling, to a life spent in making bargains, or plodding lawsuits, or swaying with gentlemanly satisfaction

the small sceptre of some decent neighbourhood, little know the treasures of grand emotion from which they shut them out, – treasures found only in preaching Jesus to the heathen ... He whose heart once heaved with the desire to live and die preaching Christ, but who, by a preference on his own part, or that of his parents, for the things precious in this life, has been withheld from the work, may sit him down and weep. He has lost what he will never regain. He lives a poorer man ... he will die with an undergrown soul, and to all eternity will lack joys and honours.[29]

Arthur here is not suggesting that heaven would be closed to some believers, but that their enjoyment of it would be less than complete due to disobedience and a failure to win souls.

Arthur's view of mission was comprehensive, encompassing both personal and social renewal. Nothing short of the renewal of society as a whole would satisfy the Christian, he held. Although of the opinion that 'the only way to the effectual regeneration of society is the regeneration of individuals', he was also quick to add that 'fearful' social evil could exist in a situation in which 'many are holy, and all have a large amount of Christian light'.[30] Serious, sustained study and effort were therefore required if social regeneration was to become a reality. Slavery, sexual abuse and other crimes against the family, racial prejudice and bad housing were all legitimate objects of Christian concern. He also recognized that in India the ties which bound people closely together were so strong as to call into question the very concept of individuality:

The whole population is cemented. No individuality exists. Each family and each caste is impacted in itself, and concreted with all the others, each person forming but a particle of the mass. A man's mind consists of the traditions of the ancients, the usages of his caste, and the dogmas of his sect: independent principles, independent convictions, independent habits, he has none.[31]

This cohesiveness which initially made individual conversions so rare and difficult, could, however, ultimately enhance the prospects of fundamental change. Resorting to the kind of scientific allusion of which he was particularly fond, he wrote:

> The missionary ... may be impatiently thinking that the solidity caused by these bonds has reflected into vacant space the impulse he had applied; while, in fact, by that very means it is transmitted through many a region unseen by him, and is even then vibrating at the core of the mass. It does seem clear, that when you have a moral force equal to effect the change designed, the more close the mutual dependency of those to be acted upon, the more wide the influence exerted by every application of that force ... To one who thinks for the present only, the peculiar features of Hindu society will appear most formidable obstacles; to one who thinks for a century, they will appear the most certain instruments of universality in the ultimate triumph.[32]

The all-pervading influence of traditionalism and the cohesiveness of Hindu society were major obstacles to individual conversion. People were understandably reluctant to turn their backs on value systems and practices they had inherited across countless centuries. Other obstacles noted by Arthur included the poor example set by other Europeans, who were automatically assumed to be Christians (mainly government officials, soldiers and traders); and the support given by trading companies to Hinduism to strengthen local links, which was interpreted as an honouring of Hinduism. Other factors included the role of Roman Catholic missions in blurring the distinctions between Christianity and Hinduism; and the radically different nature of true Christian teaching on the nature of God and the need for, and means of, salvation. These points, including the uniqueness of Christ, have already been discussed.[33] However great the obstacles and his concern that people would come to new life in Christ, Arthur was adamant that the making of disciples by compulsion – through government coercion or through material incentives – was wholly unacceptable.

Arthur was closely associated with a number of missionary initiatives at home and overseas. A cluster of these came within a few years. He was on hand at the Mission House in 1858 when steps were taken which led to fuller participation in world mission by Methodist women through the creation of The Ladies' Committee for the Amelioration of the Condition of Women in Heathen Countries. In 1860, he commended a system practiced in Bradford of raising money and arousing interest on behalf of missions through the Juvenile Missionary Association, and encouraged its adoption on a wider basis. Arthur was also a central figure in the decision to designate two missionaries for Italy in 1861. His involvement with Sir Francis Lycett, also in 1861, was crucial in establishing the Metropolitan Chapel Building Fund, an attempt to consolidate Methodist witness in British cities. Around the same time, Arthur and Lycett were supportive of the work of Josiah Cox in China, helping to smooth the way for fresh work to commence in Hankow. A visit by Arthur to Paris in the same year led to the strengthening of work at Rue Roquepine. His abiding interest in Ireland and India was also influential. For example, as early as 1848, at a public meeting in London, he proposed a scheme whereby the scriptures could be placed in every home in India in which someone could read. It is said that this had a considerable impact on Bible distribution, especially in South India through the Madras Bible Society.[34] In 1852, he supported a move to have Westport in the west of Ireland, the place of his conversion, designated as a mission area. He later contributed generously to the building of a new Methodist chapel in the town in 1875. Arthur's view, expounded in 1848, of the threefold nature of the Wesleyan Methodist Missionary Society – to the heathen, the colonies and Europe – and his belief in the interplay between missions at home and overseas, were thus amply illustrated in his own interests and activities.

Arthur resisted enforced comity arrangements, whereby different missionary societies and churches agreed among themselves to work in separate areas, as an expression of mutual acceptance and to avoid the wasting of resources. He was particularly opposed to missionary societies going behind the backs of existing churches overseas in arriving at such arrangements, as he claimed had happened in Samoa.[35] Arthur's main objection to comity arrangements was that in large cities and vast rural areas in countries such as India, the resources of one mission would simply not be sufficient to meet all the needs and opportunities. Certainly, Arthur argued, waste should be avoided, and missions should regard one another as partners in the work rather than as rivals, but co-operative efforts, to be effective, required local agreement. They should also reflect acceptance of the principle of unity-in-diversity, rather than imposed uniformity. Arthur's approach to church union was along similar lines.

Arthur recognized that the church's mission, though important, was but part of God's mission through history. This was the perspective from which he viewed and interpreted movements such as the French Revolution in 1848, the spread of British influence through colonialism, the American Civil War, the ending of slavery and political developments in Italy. With regard to the latter in 1860, he observed:

> For the moment the absorption of men's minds in political questions is unfriendly to the quiet process of awakening and conversion. And spiritually-minded men, looking up to the storm roaring over their heads, are ready to distrust it, as if it could produce no other than earthly and disturbing results ... But they forget that in every national deliverance God has been at the same time working by two distinct currents, – the silent operations of the Spirit upon the minds of individuals, and political movements, by which unconscious crowds have been led to impulses, and unwilling politicians to measures, that have issued in making the way of the Gospel free. Let not, then, the spiritually-minded Italians complain of the public turmoil.[36]

A missionary controversy stirred up in the late 1880s by a series of articles in the *Methodist Times*, and officially resolved in 1890, was particularly distressing to Arthur.[37] The articles were written by Dr H.S. Lunn, who had served for a short period as a medical missionary in India, and by Hugh Price Hughes, the editor of the *Methodist Times*. The articles challenged the ways in which it was alleged the missionary policies of the distinguished educationist, Dr Alexander Duff, had been applied. These had resulted, it was claimed, in an over-emphasis of education among privileged classes, at the expense of evangelistic and other initiatives among the masses. Yet few conversions had taken place among the privileged classes, the articles maintained, while missionaries became remote from the vast majority of Indians and from the

Indian church.[38] Charges of a luxurious life-style were levelled at Methodist and other missionaries from mainline churches. People wielding 'almost absolute power' and accustomed to receive 'abject reverence', were in danger of losing sight of the fundamental Christian principle of the brotherhood of all men, it was argued.[39] The recommended remedy was a *via media* which sought to avoid the extremes both of luxury and of asceticism. Stipends should be reduced significantly, with, however, liberal allowances for children and for health measures. Priorities should be re-assessed, and personnel re-allocated.[40]

The articles indicated sympathy with emerging nationalist thinking in India, and demonstrated social and evangelistic concern. They sparked off a wave of anti-missionary feeling in both Britain and India, which was not limited to church and mission circles. This in turn affected missionary support and the morale of missionaries. Arthur contributed to the debate, commenting that the charge of luxury was 'not worth a snap of the finger', and that in general those who had come out against established mission policy and practice had displayed 'an intensity of ignorance' and failed to produce supporting evidence.[41] He therefore added his weight to an official resolution which completely exonerated Wesleyan missionaries in India, and voiced profound regret that charges 'so grave and so unsustained' should ever have been brought against them.[42] One is left to wonder, however, whether an opportunity had not been lost to reasses policy and practice in an area in which the Christian impact had fallen far behind expectations.

Throughout his life Arthur opposed every endeavour to curtail or limit mission in any way. His convictions were as strong towards the end of the century as at any other time, as is clear from this statement in 1896:

> Some would limit mission work. No missions in Christian countries: it is an affront to a baptized people to be treated as if they were heathen. No missions where a Bishop, whether Anglican, Greek, or Roman, is in possession: it is an offence against episcopal order. No missions to Jews: they are incorrigible. No missions to Mohammedans: they are harder than the nether millstone. No missions to Buddhists: Buddhism is

better than the Gospel; and so forth. And I once heard, even
in the Methodist Conference, no missions in Roman Catholic
countries. All these limitations of mission work are vanity.[43]

Forty years earlier he had maintained that missionaries should be
sent to traditionally Christian countries in which the gospel had
been 'perverted and almost lost'.[44] To him, mission was 'the best
of causes'. The whole church was continuously called to share the
good news of Christ with all the world.

One observer has concluded that Arthur's early exposure to
Hinduism greatly sharpened his intellectual powers and helped
to develop the skills he later displayed in controversies and in the
field of apologetics.[45] It is these areas that now claim our attention.

6

Controversialist: Education

William Arthur's commitment to education grew throughout his life, as he interpreted its nature, importance and applications in the light of varying experiences. Contact with India and other 'mission countries' taught him the strategic value of education in opening up access to women and other disadvantaged groups. Work with John Scott, Wesleyan Methodism's foremost educationist, in London in the 1840s put him in touch with issues arising from church-state co-operation in education. Advocacy in London on behalf of 'ragged schools' indicated a concern to see education extended to the urban poor. Life in France in the mid- to late 1840s introduced him to the approach of education in a neighbouring European country; and his acquaintance with a scheme of national education introduced into Ireland in 1831 prompted him to view proposals for a scheme of elementary education in Britain (four decades later than the one in Ireland) in a different perspective from that of several of Wesleyan Methodism's other leading educationists. He also had some knowledge of educational developments in the United States.

When therefore Arthur approached the task of becoming Principal or President of the new Methodist College in Belfast in 1868, he did so from the vantage point of already having behind him a rich store of educational expertise despite his inexperience of formal class-room teaching. He was also fortunate in having helped to plan the college from the initial stages. The institution consisted of a 'school', catering for children of six years and upwards, and a 'college' which prepared students for adult life. The school made special provision for the children of Methodist preachers. Initially started with boys only, classes for girls were added within the first year.[1]

Arthur's inaugural address as President of Methodist College was given on 19 August 1868, and received wide local coverage.[2] Delivered without the aid of a manuscript, as an example of an applied education, the address portrayed in outline the 'liberal education' aimed at by the college's founding fathers. The range, process, method, limits and practical objectives of such an education were all introduced. Education involved the total effort from birth onwards 'to lead out the capacities of the child into the qualities' of adulthood, with the home, the school and the college each having a part to play.[3] On the role of the family and the home, Arthur incidentally noted one mark of a happy home – a mother teaching her child to laugh – and drew attention to the need for order, mental and social stimulus, and a spiritual approach to life. A problem teachers had faced in the past, he claimed good-humouredly, had been 'how to confer the maximum of drudgery with the minimum of progress'. To him there was nothing comparable to 'the joy of progress' in stimulating learning, and so attempts would be made to set achievable goals.[4] Efforts would be made to develop the pupils' powers of reasoning, comparison, expression and production. The latter, which we might more familiarly refer to as creativity, was presented as:

> that inward faculty in the human being by which he is enabled to put forth an idea of what does not exist in fact, but which is capable of being embodied in fact, and will afterwards be embodied in fact. This power, in its highest exercise, is perhaps the grandest of the human powers.

It should not be assumed, however, that 'production' was the preserve of academics only:

> Every human being has the faculty. The dairy-maid who has seized a new pattern for a pat of butter, and who brings it out into expression, has really given birth to a new thought. And so on until you come to that exertion of this power whereby the mind can conceive a poem, an oration, or a palace, which it can build within the soul before it has ever received physical form or beauty.[5]

Poetry, art and natural science could all help to develop this power, Arthur claimed. It may be noted at this point that the existence of a commercial department in the upper school, teaching such subjects as penmanship, book-keeping, and the principles and history of commerce, was evidence of a desire to meet the needs of a wide range of pupils.

Arthur underlined the practical side of education. To the question as to why boys should be educated, he replied simply that it was to make men of them. That, he claimed, was 'the whole philosophy of education in one word'.[6] Education which failed to lead people to engage in good and useful activities was flawed, he insisted. On specialization, Arthur held that it should be the aim of a college or university first to teach their students the elements of many subjects. This was not to make them 'smatterers in many things', but to help them to appreciate 'something of everything' before they discovered and followed up areas of specialist interest.[7] The explosion of knowledge in the twentieth century, in new and technical areas as well as in traditional fields of study, will, in the view of some people, have made it impossible to delay specialization in this way.

Questions relating to Wesleyan Methodism's educational policies and those of the state came to the fore during Arthur's years in Belfast. He keenly felt his remoteness from London, but entered the debate as far as distance would allow through personal and public correspondence. His friend James Rigg was now at the heart of affairs in Britain, having moved to the education desk within Wesleyan Methodism. Rigg strongly believed in maintaining the voluntary principle wherever possible, but he accepted that it could not cope with the needs of the entire nation. He therefore sketched a plan combining voluntary and municipal efforts under government control, along lines similar to those later placed before Parliament in W.E. Forster's Education Bill.[8] A special and unusually large committee of more than two hundred and fifty ministers and laity had been appointed by the Wesleyan Methodist Conference in 1869 in view of the anticipated Bill. It met in November before Forster introduced his Bill to Parliament, and the following May there was a three-day discussion on the details of the Bill. Rigg's main concern was the position adopted by his oldest and dearest ministerial friend, William Arthur. As early as December 1868 Arthur had warned, 'Set every one on the watch against denominational education in Ireland. It will be worse than endowing the Priests.'[9] On 23

October 1869, he explained his position at length to Rigg, out of concern that his views be represented to the special committee meeting the following month. This is such an important letter that it is quoted at length:

> The Denominational system is friendly to Popery & to High Churchism, & shuts up Methodism to certain localities. If perpetuated it will destroy our agricultural circuits; & will proportionately train the agricultural population to Anti-Protestant feeling.
>
> Free schools for all is the thing to go for. If we do so it can be carried, & the reading of the Bible publicly in the school too, with separate religious teaching at set times by ministers of different denominations . . . Such a system wd. give us a fair chance of holding our own in Cornwall, & other large & poor populations. It would open to our influence schools wherever we had ministers. It would effectively baulk Tractarian & Romish claims . . . To go in for 'supplementing the Denominational system', & for making state aid to education in some sort analogous to outdoor relief is not only shortsighted, but a public wrong. The nation will have schools; ought to have them free; & in time will. We may hinder it long enough to secure the final triumph of the secular principle; but if we go for the interests of all, we shall best promote our own.[10]

Days later he followed up with further letters, reiterating similar points. 'Free Bible Schools' were what they should go for, he urged. They were attainable, would save the education department from having to engage in sectarian fighting, and would open up the way for Methodists to play a part in educational boards. Methodists had it in their power to influence the course of events since, he claimed, the denominational system would die without their support. Rigg had been wholly wrong, he complained, to commit himself to a policy before his committee had met. 'If ever you made a damaging mistake in your life', wrote Arthur to his friend, 'you are doing it now'. At the same time Arthur recognized that his was a minority position and ran counter to the mood of the times. 'Even if I stand alone', he concluded, 'I shall go for the course I believe to be well for us and for the nation'.[11] At the protracted meeting of the committee in May 1870, Arthur used all his powers of persuasion to encourage acceptance of a resolution which would have sought to safeguard the rights of existing denominational schools without adding to their number under the new legislation.[12] The move failed, however, and a deputation was appointed to meet Mr Gladstone to submit the committee's resolutions, including the concern that no by-law should prohibit scriptural reading and instruction.

In March 1871, Arthur commented in a letter to Rigg that the educational disadvantages of non-Anglicans were very great, and would be difficult to redress. He was still opposed 'to Dr Pusey's plan of denominational Colleges'.[13] A further letter followed on 25 October in which he remarked that on that very day Rigg was probably on his way to the School Board in London 'to plead for the payment of fees in Denominational Schools out of rates'. This would place Arthur in a moral dilemma:

> If you tax me for that purpose the payment will be made with a protest of conscience & a revulsion of judgment such as I have never felt in any payment for national uses. I shall feel myself compelled by law & force to pay for the efficient endowment of all kinds of religions, & that with a pretext of not doing it; to pay for the most effective opposition possible to my own religious views & denomination; to pay for the discouragement of sects which foster self-reliance & the subsidising of those which breed pauperism, to pay for encouragement to a system of extremes, one which on the one hand takes the money of the wealthy & on the other bribes the pauper, & uses both against those who are neither rich nor dependent but what is the bulk our people are. Greater inequality than this . . . I can hardly fancy.[14]

At a meeting of the committee in December 1872, Arthur made another attempt to stem the tide by proposing, much as he had done at the previous Conference, that the denominational system should be gradually merged 'in one of united unsectarian schools, with the Bible, under School Boards'.[15] Not surprisingly this was strongly resisted, being pronounced in one quarter as 'totally and absolutely impracticable'. Rigg himself held that, if carried, Arthur's proposal would have damaged the work of his department irreparably by discouraging the natural growth of Methodist schools.[16] Others saw Arthur's attitude as a threat to existing Methodist educational institutions. He strongly denied this at a meeting of the committee the following year, arguing that he favoured a system whereby Methodists and others could subscribe to support their own work. He objected to public money being used for denominational schools whose religious principles many did not embrace.[17] This echoed the stance taken by many Nonconformists, among whom the Congregationalist R.W. Dale played a prominent part.[18] In 1871, they had turned their attention to the twenty-fifth clause of Forster's Education Bill, which provided that children born in poor law institutions should be sent to school as a charge on the rates. This became a cause of annoyance when the school was a denominational one. The only vested interest the state system should uphold, argued Arthur, was that of parents and their children, and other children under the protection of school boards in unsectarian schools:

> We should take our stand, not beside the great and powerful, the titled and the dignified, who claim to control by their money the education of our working men and working women's children; but beside our own working men and working women, and those of Primitive Methodists, and say, 'We will go for the parent's right; we will go for the extension of schoolboards everywhere'.[19]

In the end the committee resolved that Methodist schools and training colleges should be maintained 'in full vigour and efficiency',[20] and that primary schools provided wholly out of the public purse should be on the principle of unsectarian schools under school boards. The Methodist Conference fully endorsed the committee's findings and recorded its

> deliberate conviction that, in justice to the interests of national education in the broadest sense, and to the religious denominations in the country, School Boards should be established everywhere, and an undenominational school placed within reasonable distance of every family.[21]

Neither Rigg nor Arthur could claim an outright victory, though the former had more cause for satisfaction. Henry Rack has pointed out that 'the passions and policies' within Methodism reflected a much wider issue, namely the entrance of Nonconformity into the mainstream of British life, with the moral and religious tensions this aroused.[22] It could also be argued that many of the points made have a bearing on today's debate about providing schools for religious and other minorities. They also provide an interesting comparison with ideas fundamental to the recent establishment of integrated schools in Northern Ireland.

Rigg felt Arthur's opposition on educational policy deeply, though their friendship held fast. In August 1870, following the meeting of the Wesleyan Methodist Conference, Rigg confided to his brother that he had had to differ sharply with Arthur on the issue, and had 'even in a sense to set him down', which had been deeply distressing.[23] Twenty-five years later he reflected on the controversy in a letter to Dr Benson, the Archbishop of Canterbury, in which he expressed support for Anglican schools while indicating his rejection of aspects of Anglican belief and practice:

> There was a powerful section antagonistic to denominational day schools, a section headed at that time by a very dear friend of mine; one who, for his eloquence, his nobility of character, and his general ability, was the first man in our Church – the Rev. William Arthur . . . It taxed to the utmost all our courage, resolution, and powers of discussion to repulse at that time the attack which Mr Arthur led. We did repulse it, but the old leaven has never ceased to work, and the increasing intensity of alienation from the Church of England which has shown itself in the party politics and votes of Methodists, finds vent also in antagonism to Anglican day schools.
>
> All this I deeply regret, but such are the conditions with which we have to deal. For myself, much as I deplore sacerdotal excesses in doctrine and practice and parochial assumptions and exclusiveness, I should regard it as a grievous calamity if the day schools of the Church of England were destroyed.[24]

Not content with expressing his opposition to the direction of events within Methodism, Arthur also sought to mount an attack on related national issues in education through a series of letters

to the editor of the *Daily News* in 1869. These gave further
evidence of his opposition to high Anglicanism and Roman
Catholicism, particularly in Ireland. This, more than anything
else, accounted for the parting of the ways with Rigg and others
on education. They inevitably viewed matters primarily from the
point of view of Britain's needs, where Roman Catholicism posed
less of a threat than in Ireland. Arthur regarded them from the
stand-point of their likely impact on evangelical witness in Ireland,
which he believed would be disastrous. In proposing that the
English system of denominational education be extended to
Ireland, the Irish bishops were, according to Arthur in the first
letter in the series, being less than honest. Features in England
included the need to raise at least two-thirds of the costs of
schools; a prohibition on ecclesiastical persons teaching (priests,
ministers and even lay preachers); and a conscience clause to
protect the religious beliefs of minorities. There was also an
insistence that teachers hold certificates of qualification, that
payment of grants be on results not numbers, and that inspectors
be of another denomination. None of these points, argued Arthur,
was likely to be accepted by the Irish bishops; yet failure to accept
them would alter the English system beyond recognition. The
bishops were seeking funds from the nation, and control by
themselves.[25] The *Irish Evangelist* fully endorsed Arthur's stance
in February 1869, using emotive phrases such as 'the smooth talk'
of the bishops, 'the dogmas and mummeries of Popery', and 'a
Protestant nation'. Fair play by English standards, not Irish
'Popish privilege and ascendancy', was what was needed. The
problem of national education in Ireland was insoluble, except
through 'a system of education strictly and purely secular'.[26] It is
difficult to avoid the impression that this 'solution' was mainly
the product of fear of Roman Catholicism. It should also be noted
that Arthur's proposal for England, 'united unsectarian schools',
was a modification of the Irish system with the addition of the
phrase 'with the Bible'. Talk of a system 'strictly and purely
secular' was misleading.

The distinction between 'education' and 'instruction', made
in the 'united secular education, separate religious instruction'
formula, though not absolute, could be significant. Arthur does
not seem to have discussed to what extent the instructional

element in religion is responsible for forming and encouraging myths, positively about one's 'own side' and negatively about the 'other side'. He was, however, aware of the possibility of slanted views, for example about history, being communicated and greatly feared that this would be the tendency in denominational schools in which Catholic authorities were responsible for appointments, the selection of text-books and inspections. But he did not take the point that history as traditionally presented reflected a bias in the direction of what was pro-British and pro-Protestant, anti-Irish and anti-Roman Catholic.

In the second letter to the *Daily News* Arthur examined proposals to the government by the Catholic bishops in Ireland, suggesting adjustments to the national system of education in Ireland.[27] Submitted to Sir George Grey, the Home Secretary, in 1862, these were passed on to the Board of Commissioners in Dublin who, properly, pleaded their own non-political status. The proposals then appeared in parliamentary papers in March 1866. Arthur's response came in 1869, as he established himself in Belfast, and the proposals found their way through a bureaucratic labyrinth and survived changes on the political scene. The bishops divided national schools into ordinary and model, and asked that all ordinary schools (whether vested or non-vested) in which the children of only one denomination were enrolled, should be regarded as 'denominational' rather than 'mixed'. In such 'Catholic' schools, the bishops, according to Arthur, argued that religious education should be blended with secular, Catholic teachers and inspectors should be appointed, books should be approved by Catholic authorities, and there should be no restriction on religious emblems and exercises. The bishops further held that, unlike in England, the state should provide the funds for future denominational schools as it did for existing national schools, on account of Ireland's economic disadvantages. The bishops also declared themselves wholly opposed to model schools. These had been introduced from 1847 onwards, with the aim of demonstrating improved methods of instruction and training teachers. Built and administered by the Board of Commissioners, they denied to Catholic bishops (and to leaders in the other denominations) a direct say in the appointment of teachers or the selection of books.

Arthur's response to the bishops was to claim, in line with his earlier letter, that under the guise of 'levelling up' the schools in Ireland, they were advocating at almost every point a different system from the one in England. He praised the model schools uncritically, claiming that they offered a necessary combination of united secular education and separate religious instruction. He must have known, however, that there had been a series of alleged abuses in the schools, with charges of Protestant proselytism and the distortion of Catholic belief and practice. Some of these charges had been sustained, heightening Catholic fears and leading to official Catholic action against the schools. At best the schools were regarded by many Catholics as secular, at worst as subtle de-Catholicizing agents. Arthur's most telling point was when he highlighted the plight of the Protestant minority in parts of Ireland, if the bishops had their way:

> Where the minority were not strong enough – as in the south and west of Ireland would be everywhere the case – to set up a school against the State one, they would have for alternative to keep their children from school, or to have the money and authority of the nation, under direction of the Roman Catholic Bishop, used to make their schooling the means of proselytising them. The whole south and west of Ireland would thus have a monkish education fastened upon it. The schoolmaster would be under the parish priest and the inspector; the priest and inspector would be under the Bishop; the Bishop under Cardinal Cullen, and he under the Pope.[28]

As often in Ireland, each side failed to appreciate the other's perception, and fear faced fear.

Arthur's third letter[29] contained a topical reference to the imminent disestablishment of the Church of Ireland. When one national endowment was in process of being abolished because some felt 'it excited sectarian hatred', it would not be appropriate to replace another which had been introduced in part to lessen sectarianism, namely the national system of education, with one which would bequeath sectarian bitterness to later generations. His anticipation of what might emerge if the bishops' demands were conceded made grim reading. Every other religious grouping could also demand denominational schools, with the state having to bear most costs; ecclesiastical, uncertified, persons as teachers; no conscience clause; grants for books even when they carried a slanted view of history, for example; payment of grants by numbers not results; and denominational inspectors. Only one other scenario could be more divisive, he conjectured. This was that one part of the country be placed under Protestant schools, in which sectarian feeling had been fanned by recent conflict; with the other part placed under schools taught by Catholic orders and laity. Christian duty and political interest required that religion be expressed in ways likely to reduce, not inflame, animosity; and the signs were still good for united secular education with separate religious instruction. The majority of lay people, Protestant and Catholic, would accept 'mixed' schools, whose numbers were increasing, were it not for clerical opposition which was particularly strong on the Catholic side. The bishops' stance was more expressive of 'ultramontane power' than of concern for Catholic lay people. Yet the Queen's Colleges and national schools had already achieved much in training people 'in the Christian duty of honouring all men' and in the 'English' virtue of having respect for the consciences of others. The national system was indeed in need of modification, Arthur acknowledged, but this should be in the direction of making it more national and less denominational.

Arthur here seems to have been indulging in wishful thinking. Catholics progressively stopped using the model schools in the North during the 1860s,[30] and aggravation at Queen's College, Belfast, from 1866 to 1867 had an unsettling effect on Catholics. The line that Catholic laity were generally reasonable and accepting of the national scheme in its present form, and that the problem lay basically with their priests and bishops, was a standard position adopted by some Protestants on a range of issues. It did not, however, correspond with reality when viewed from a Catholic perspective, and certainly could not provide a sufficient basis on which an acceptable scheme for the future could be worked out.

In April 1870, the *Irish Evangelist* welcomed the formation of a National Education League for Ireland.[31] This sought to maintain and develop non-sectarian education in Ireland, to raise the status of teachers and improve the quality of education in the national schools. The fact, however, that prominent Protestants who were known to be militantly anti-Roman Catholic supported the League, was to accelerate the opposite process. In the same article in the *Irish Evangelist* a further letter by Arthur to the English press, written the previous month, was quoted approvingly. In this Arthur raised objections to the Education Bill, claiming that Forster had exaggerated the influence of both denominationalists and secularists. He had also, according to Arthur, underestimated the strength of feeling of those who wanted schools where the Bible had a place and which yet were unsectarian. The Bill smacked of French, indeed anti-English, 'latitudinarianism of the present denominational system, combined with a religious despotism of majorities pregnant with civil contention'. Arthur's solution, predictably, lay with Ireland's model school system. As before, its virtues were extolled without reference to criticisms of it within Ireland:

> In such schools religion is not bound, not ignored, not imposed; no one is obliged to pay for the religion of another, or to learn what he does not believe, or buy for his child secular education at the expense of religious conviction. With such a solution of the religious difficulty ready tested, surely we are not forced either on secularism or on the absolute will of a majority liable to an annual change.

The success of the model schools depended, however, on a high level of sensitivity on the part of teachers, and inevitably there were failures in Ireland with performance falling below what was required. There were, for example, instances in which zealous Protestant teachers gave anti-Roman Catholic instruction to both Protestant and Catholic children.[32] From a Catholic point of view, the success of the schools would have depended also on sufficient numbers of qualified and recognized Catholic teachers being available to give religious instruction. The chances of this happening in Ireland lessened as attitudes hardened and Catholic authorities withdrew official support from the model schools.

In Arthur's approach to education, the aim of setting achievable goals for pupils, the recognition of the importance of creativity, and the attempt to meet the needs of a variety of students, were healthy emphases. In his clash with Rigg over Wesleyan and national educational policies, his basic contention that the churches rather than the state should be responsible for promoting and maintaining denominational schools, was sound. Valid too was his acknowledgment of the inconsistency in pressing for state support for Methodist denominational education, while denying the same right to Roman Catholics and high Anglicans. His letters in the *Daily News* drew attention to departures from the English system in the proposals by the Irish Roman Catholic hierarchy. His chief educational achievement lay in ensuring a successful launch for Methodist College.

One writer has claimed that no satisfactory system of national education could be introduced in nineteenth-century Europe except where one form of religion was dominant, or where a government was strong enough to override denominational dissatisfaction, or where there was an established tradition of inter-denominational co-operation.[33] Another writer has added more recently that it could also have been achieved through what he termed 'the back door of bureaucratic encroachment', or where a religious consensus emerged through fear of the alternatives.[34] The discussion in this chapter has drawn attention to the strength of feelings, and to the complexity of the issues, involved when the churches played their part in the national debate on education in Britain and Ireland in the 1860s and 1870s. Although recognizing the growing need for the government to become more directly involved in helping to provide a more widely available system of education on a national level, the churches differed sharply on the part to be played by denominational schools in such a system. Had religion been regarded more as a peripheral matter, or the differences between the churches perceived as less important, responsible compromise would have been less difficult. It proved impossible, however, 'on matters which meant life or death to the State as well as heaven and hell to the individual'.[35]

D.W. Bebbington has pointed out that the national controversy over education subsided for twenty years from the mid–1870s.[36] One factor in this was the repeal in 1876 of the twenty-fifth clause of the 1870 Act. Foreign affairs became a growing concern, but it was the Irish Home Rule controversy which emerged as the dominant national issue.

7

Controversialist: Politics

D.W. Bebbington has indicated three features of 'the Noncon-formist conscience' which emerged during the 1870s and 1880s, which are directly relevant to our concern. These were a conviction that there was no strict division between religion and politics, an insistence that politicians should be people of the highest personal moral character, and a belief that the state should promote the moral welfare of its citizens.[1] William Arthur, while holding to the 'no politics' tradition within Wesleyan Methodism, broadly embraced these points. Methodists, he argued, could neither align themselves exclusively with one particular political party nor stand aloof from political debate. Methodist ministers, whatever the practice in other churches, he maintained, should not appear on political platforms. Yet, he argued, it was essential for them to make their views known on moral, social and religious questions while taking care not to commit the church as such. This, it seemed clear to Arthur, was entirely consistent with the denomination's traditional stance on slavery, education, alcohol and the opium trade.[2] Arthur himself became directly involved, sometimes con-troversially, in commenting on such matters as political develop-ments, race, education and the role of the press. It was, however, W.E. Gladstone's Home Rule policy for Ireland which thrust Arthur, late in life, even more into fierce public debate.

After the imprisonment of the Irish Land League leaders, C.S. Parnell used his parliamentary party to help to defeat and dismiss from office Gladstone's Liberal government which had already become unpopular due to its failure to relieve General Gordon at Khartoum in 1884. Prior to the election in 1885, Arthur published an anti-Parnell pamphlet, *The Householder's Parliament*, in which he drew attention to the responsibility democratic reform had placed on an increasing number of adults, making the family the decisive unit of legislative power. It was therefore imperative, he urged, that voters ensured that those who were elected, whether within the ruling party or in opposition, respected the fundamental democratic principle of 'power of action to the majority and power of criticism to the minority'.[3] Factious opposition and time-wasting blocking procedures, such as had been practised by Parnell and his followers in their obstructionist policy, prevented Parliament from fulfilling its proper function.

The general election of 1885 returned a Parliament in which the Liberal members equalled the total of Conservatives plus Parnellite Irish. Driven by political necessity, Conservatives and Liberals both talked to Parnell, but it was Gladstone who came to accept the need for Home Rule, as a means to promote peace and stability in Ireland. When his 'conversion' was announced, most Conservatives declared themselves against the measure and the defeat of Salisbury's government soon followed. In February 1886, Gladstone formed his third cabinet with the intention of introducing Home Rule. For the following decade the Irish question became the key issue in British politics.

Gladstone's first Home Rule Bill proposed a Legislative Body in Dublin to deal with Irish affairs in subordination to the Imperial Parliament at Westminster. The Irish Parliament, composed of two 'Orders', was forbidden to make laws relating to such matters as the crown, foreign relations and war. It fell short of nationalist demands, but Parnell and the Irish Party accepted it in principle, reserving the right to seek amendment in detail. Particularly contentious from a Unionist point of view was the proposal, not changed till the second Bill, that Irish members would no longer sit at Westminster. The Bill was rejected in Parliament in June 1886, a split in the Liberal party playing a decisive part in this, with the two extreme wings, the Whigs and the radicals, withholding support from Gladstone.

Much of the following six years was devoted by Gladstone to an attempt to convince the British electorate that to grant Home Rule to Ireland would be an act of justice and wisdom. His association with Parnell continued until late in 1890 when, against the background of controversy following the O'Shea divorce and the split within Parnell's party, it became clear that any continuing alliance with Parnell would be politically damaging.[4] Gladstone formed his fourth cabinet in August 1892, its members held together mainly through awe of him. His second Home Rule Bill was introduced the following year, and differed significantly from the first. It provided for continued Irish representation at Westminster, and proposed an Irish Parliament in which the single-chamber device with its 'Orders' was dropped, with the right of appeal to the House of Lords if there was dissatisfaction over any measure of the Irish Parliament. Gladstone himself piloted the Bill through eighty-five sittings of the House of Commons, but it was rejected in the House of Lords by the largest majority recorded to that point, 419 to 41.

Nonconformists in Britain had come to regard Gladstone as a highly principled and deeply religious leader. They had no history of support for Home Rule prior to Gladstone's change of heart. On the contrary, they viewed the measure with deep suspicion as a policy mainly of disloyal and illiberal Roman Catholics who, given the opportunity, would do their utmost to crush Irish Protestantism. It is therefore a remarkable tribute to Gladstone's personal standing and persuasive powers that he was able to retain the confidence of the majority of Nonconformists in Britain and gain acceptance by them of his first Home Rule Bill. Despite the Bill's rejection and the subsequent defeat of the Liberal Government, most Nonconformists in Britain became and remained convinced Home Rulers. The major elements in this change of outlook were their traditional loyalty to Liberalism and their continuing trust in Gladstone.

In Ireland, however, things were very different, with the major Protestant churches and organizations speaking with one voice in opposition to Gladstone's proposals. An Irish Methodist source in June 1886 pointed out that the Church of Ireland, and the Presbyterian, Non-Subscribing Presbyterian, Wesleyan, Primitive Methodist, Methodist New Connexion and Moravian Churches had all come out strongly against Home Rule.[5] Opponents in the churches joined with others elsewhere, often using similar arguments. A recent survey of some thirty Ulster unionist speeches[6] shows that in descending order of priority the arguments used were as follows. An ascendant Roman Catholicism would persecute the Protestant community, and Ulster Protestants would lose their imperial heritage and have a reduced status in the world.

Catholic nationalists, who were no respecters of law, order and industry, would reduce a prosperous Ulster to ruin. Home Rule was a betrayal of loyalism, and Ulster would be compelled to meet the major portion of Ireland's contribution to the British Exchequer. All were agreed that the old pattern of agitation, coercion and concession, which had been true of Irish nationalist and British relations up to that point in the nineteenth century, had now come to an end. What was at stake in 1886 was nothing less than the future destiny of Ireland, with the nationalist and Roman Catholic majority being empowered to shape and control it. Inevitably, it was believed, politically motivated violence, of which many had direct experience, would become more persistent and widespread.

The pages of the *Christian Advocate* repeatedly voiced Irish Wesleyan Methodist concern and protest. In December 1885, a stern editorial expressed alarm at reports of proposals for Home Rule, describing nationalism as 'the spawn of an alien creed', counselling against a policy of appeasement towards nationalists, warning that Ulster would never acquiesce in Home Rule, and claiming that Home Rule was inconsistent with the integrity of the Empire.[7] Opposition rose to a crescendo in 1886. An editorial in January alleged that Home Rule for Ireland meant not only war against the crown rights of England but 'war against the Crown rights of Christ'. Home Rule, it continued:

> means the ruin of the country. Its inspiration is religious antipathy, its methods plunder, its object Protestant annihilation. Education has not asked for it, property has not sought it, commerce has not beckoned it to come. The Churches shrink from it as life from a serpent ... Under Home Rule there would be an exodus of substance.[8]

A week later an editorial highlighted the solidarity of Christian opinion in Ireland against Home Rule, conveniently ignoring the Roman Catholic Church in its comment that 'the three greatest Churches in Ireland' were of one mind on the issue. The whole of nationalist opinion was also disregarded in the remark that 'the feeling of the entire country' was one of opposition.[9]

Also in January a meeting took place of the Committee of Privileges, the body which between annual Wesleyan Methodist

Conferences expressed Irish Wesleyan Methodist opinion on public issues. Although careful to protect its independence of political parties, it affirmed Wesleyan Methodist loyalty to the United Kingdom, and declared its view that any weakening of the link with Britain would not be in Ireland's moral or material interests. Such a development would heighten, not lessen, unrest within the country.[10] This in turn sparked off a debate within the church as to the meaning of loyalty and whether the Committee had exceeded its powers and taken sides on a political question. The debate continued until the annual Wesleyan Conference in June, when by a strong majority the actions of the Committee were endorsed.[11] Those who favoured the stance of the Committee were able to point out that, on earlier occasions, the Conference itself had sworn loyalty to the crown and had deprecated attempts to loosen Ireland's links with Britain. 'The policy approved by Methodism is now declared authoritatively to be UNION', announced an editorial in the *Christian Advocate*.[12] Those who thought differently, including Jeremiah Jordan, an Irish Methodist Member of Parliament, were a small minority.

This was the background against which William Arthur's pamphlet *Shall the Loyal be Deserted?* made its appearance in 1886. An enthusiastic review claimed that it contained 'the heart of Methodism'.[13] Arthur's starting point was that of a person who thought of himself as a British citizen and regarded the United Kingdom as a single entity with a parliament, a government and a legislature. Home Rulers, on the other hand, were seen as those who were essentially trying to end the Union under which Ireland had for decades enjoyed unprecedented peace and prosperity. According to Arthur, Gladstone's proposals were grossly unfair, depriving loyal Irish of their birthright as British citizens and placing them under the rule of the Irish National League. Everyone in Ireland, nationalist and loyalist alike, was entitled to the same rights, protection and degree of self-government as citizens in other parts of the Union, Arthur argued. What Gladstone proposed, however, was to favour nationalists at the expense of loyalists. The Bill amounted to an attempt to create 'an isolated Ireland on the ground of exceptional privilege and virtual ecclesiastical dominion'.[14] Giving three and a half million 'discontented Irish' the power to 'repeal all laws, make new ones, and levy taxes', with the backing of the Empire's troops to force Irish loyalists into subjection, placed all in such peril, according to Arthur, that only divine providence could prevent civil war. Among loyalists few were keen to engage in fighting, Arthur claimed, but many held that the utmost vigilance was required. Thirty million people in other parts of the Union could admittedly force their will on one million Irish loyalists, but what had the loyalists done to deserve such coercion? They had committed no crimes, and nationalists had certainly not done anything to merit such a radical reversal in their favour.[15]

Arthur totally rejected the suggestion that there was an analogy between the opposition voiced by the loyal Irish and that expressed by the 'British Party' in some colonies in which a degree of devolved administration had been proposed. The situation was not at all comparable, he contended. Whereas colonies had been in the pupillage of the Colonial Office, and the proposal was that they be given a form of limited representation, Ireland had for eighty-six years enjoyed, as of right, direct representation in the Imperial Parliament.[16]

Arthur acknowledged that Gladstone's Bill did not technically lead to a repeal of the Union, but with others he was convinced that it dealt it a fatal blow. Had it led directly to repeal, the damage done through the proposals could perhaps have been lessened, since more effective steps could be taken to safeguard the Empire. As it was, the 'guarantees' contained within the Bill were worthless, placing trust in those who were utterly unreliable, namely Parnell and his associates.[17] Arthur was sharply critical of Gladstone's assessment of people and his skill in taking political initiatives:

> From the first I heard him argue a case – that of the admission of the Jews to Parliament – I felt that . . . his intellect was an enigma: breadth and elevation of view, depth of feeling, justice of intention, consummate subtlety of analysis and flexibility of expression; but – but a mode of judging, now direct, now oblique, essentially fitful, not to say wayward.[18]

In private correspondence, though still appreciative of Gladstone's strengths, for example in finance and management, Arthur was less restrained in indicating his weaknesses. Gladstone's mistaken judgment, apparent in the earlier controversy over education, was evident again:

> How Lord Salisbury must bless Gladstone & those who encouraged him! This is the second time that by a sudden movement he has jolted the Liberal Party out of gear. While he followed on the lines traced by the sounder heads of the party – I do not mean more capacious or more luminous – he was splendid to advocate, & manage; but when he takes to initiating whether legislating or administering, he is just as liable to go wrong as right. Cobden & Bright could initiate safely, Trevelyan can administer safely & soundly, but except in pure finance, what Gladstone will do in a given case, is a toss up ... The Liberal party, in his hand has been shattered![19]

Arthur's distrust of Roman Catholicism, particularly its priests, is evident throughout the pamphlet. For example, he frequently referred to the controlling influence which he believed was exercised by priests in local branches of the Irish National League.[20] The likely outworking of the proposed Bill in the religious sphere was therefore a matter of the gravest concern. Whereas, he pointed out, the fourth clause forbade the Irish Legislature to establish a particular church, a section in the nineteenth clause provided a loophole if the assent of Her Majesty in Council could be obtained:

> That is the manner of legislation which Englishmen are to register as English, which Liberals are to be excommunicated if they do not register as Liberal, and to which Nonconformists are expected to say Amen ... So the separated Irish are not to establish a religion, but may subsidize one in the first year; and that done, the next step will need nothing but threats in Ireland, and tremblers in office here (England).[21]

It would not be long, according to Arthur, before those who were not to establish Roman Catholicism in Ireland would argue that they could not then be expected to maintain Anglicanism in England. This would set in motion a process whereby Catholicism would inevitably receive support, confirming the opinion of opponents of the Bill who from the beginning held that Gladstone was replacing one ascendancy in Ireland by another.

Grattan's Parliament had in the late eighteenth century encouraged violence and misfortune in Ireland, Arthur insisted. The Union, on the other hand, had led to an era of unparalleled prosperity. Break it up, he argued, and 'wars and distresses, weeping and wailing' would return.[22] To Arthur, therefore, the issues could not be more clear. Gladstone depended on Nonconformist support. True Liberals and Nonconformists should therefore use their influence to urge him to alter his policy on Home Rule. In doing this they would serve the best interests of Ireland and of the Empire as a whole. 'The storm birds are on the wing', he declared ominously. An evil counsel had troubled the realm, but it should not be allowed to prevail.[23]

As well as writing the pamphlet, Arthur continued to press his views in other ways. A statement by him in *The Times* in June 1886 was also released separately as a poster. As before, the benefits of the Union were extolled, and what was envisaged in Home Rule deplored:

> It is now proposed that we shall have two Parliaments, and moreover, what at the worst of times before the Union we never had, two Governments. This would lead to rival tariffs. Two clashing Parliaments, two clashing Governments, and two rival tariffs, with a paper union, in a fantastic constitution, would, as far as I can foresee, result in the ruin of Ireland and the weakening of England, as well as in the commencement of disastrous commotion in India, and of disruption in the Empire. How any man who values religious liberty can vote for handing Ireland over to the Parnellite rule is to me a moral mystery beyond all soundings.[24]

In speaking out in such forthright terms, Arthur recognized that it might be considered he had overstepped the mark of what was acceptable in Wesleyan Methodism. He therefore took the precaution of preparing an Explanation, to be read if necessary at the Wesleyan Conference in Britain in 1886, in defence of his stand. In the event, no question was raised about his conduct. James Rigg subsequently published the Explanation believing it possessed an importance beyond the immediate issues. Arthur placed his actions against the background of Methodism's 'no politics' tradition:

As to our rules, I know of none forbidding a minister to write on a public question which he believes to involve the interests of morality or religion. Nor did I ever know that so to write was disallowed by any understanding. I did understand that we were to refrain from party action, or from action in our capacity as Wesleyan Ministers. That is the rule by which I sought to walk; by which I still believe that I did walk . . . As to party action, I have understood that to mean either working with and for a party in matters where no manifest interest of religion or morals was involved, or else to mean supporting measures if proposed by one's own party, which one would resist if proposed by the other, or the reverse of this . . . All along I firmly intended to do no act as a Wesleyan Minister, but only in my citizen capacity as William Arthur.[25]

It is worth noting that Arthur did not consider membership of a political party to be an issue. In public correspondence he took care to supply only his name, without reference to status. When, however, some of his private correspondence was published without permission, or when his statements were re-published by others in unapproved forms, these conventions were sometimes flouted, causing distress and annoyance to Arthur and others.[26]

Sharp differences over Home Rule emerged among Methodists in Britain. Wesleyans formed the backbone of Nonconformist Unionism. In Lincolnshire, for example, the English county with the second highest proportion of Wesleyans, there was a large swing from Liberalism to Unionism between 1885 and 1892. In Devon and Cornwall, where Wesleyans were also numerous, the swing against Liberalism was twice the national average over that same period. Prominent Wesleyan businessmen also took a lead in rejecting Gladstone's Home Rule proposals, which were viewed as too radical.[27] On the other side, however, the new and vigorous *Methodist Times* attempted to force the issue and enthusiastically supported Gladstone, declaring that Methodists must show Christian love and ensure justice for Ireland through support for Home Rule.[28] The Irish reaction to this was predictable, and a heading appeared in the *Christian Advocate* in January 1886 – 'The Methodist Times (so called)'.[29] The following month the silence of the older, more conservative, *Methodist Recorder* was regretted – it later came out against Home Rule – and the stance of the *Methodist Times*, 'our enemy', was deplored.[30] In April an appeal was made to 'the reason, conscience and love of right' among fellow-Methodists in Britain. Whatever happens, the Irish paper declared robustly in 1888, Irish Methodists 'will not follow a senile statesman in his apostacy any more than they will join the Parnellites in rebellion and moonlighting'.[31] Irish anger was especially directed at Hugh Price Hughes, editor of the *Methodist Times* and leading exponent of Nonconformist views on social and political questions. He declared in 1888 that Home Rule was 'one form of the Golden Rule' and 'simply applied Christianity'.[32]

All of this caused immense distress to Arthur, so long a central figure in Wesleyan Methodism in Britain and an ardent promoter of Methodist links across the Irish Sea. His *Moral Points in the Home Rule Controversy*, originally published as a letter in *The Times* in 1891, indicated that there was no lessening in the strength of his feelings. Written in the aftermath of Parnell's legal dispute with *The Times* over his alleged complicity in crimes and in the light of the O'Shea affair, it was re-issued and given wide circulation by the leading unionist organization in Ireland, the Irish Loyal and Patriotic Union. Arthur made it clear that in his view events had totally vindicated the unionist position. 'I always insisted', he wrote, 'that Mr Parnell was a wholesale trader in crime; that by crime he made his power and made money, and that complicity with him was complicity with crime.'[33] Warming to his conclusion, he again pressed the benefits of the Union and declared on behalf of unionists:

> We shall not let go our Imperial franchise. We shall not be put under a Parliament in Dublin. The Imperial franchise and all which that guarantees is our birthright. No man shall take it from us. We will never sell it. If Englishmen and Scotchmen will not let us live and die in the freedom we were born to, they will have to come and kill us.[34]

It should be noted that here and at other times, in public and private, Arthur refused to endorse violent loyalist reaction. In 1886, he responded to rioting in Belfast, prompted by Home Rule agitation, by insisting that it injured the Protestant cause. Later, in conversation in London with a friend from Belfast, he condemned threats of Protestant violence in the knowledge that other people in Britain were giving more positive signals to Irish loyalists on this issue.[35]

In 1892, at a time of election fever, Arthur appealed to his ministerial colleagues at the Irish Methodist Conference not to accept invitations to address political meetings in Britain on the Home Rule issue. This, he argued, was in line with their 'no politics' tradition.[36] His words may have discouraged some from going, but others proceeded to England and the *Christian Advocate* provided extensive coverage of what they said.[37]

Guinness Rogers, a prominent Ulster-born Congregationalist and leading political commentator in Britain, gave strong support for Gladstone's proposals in his pamphlet *The Ulster Problem* (1886). In it he rejected the main thrust of Arthur's arguments, accusing him of a total lack of objectivity, gross misrepresentation and unfair assumptions.[38] The contrast between 'the Loyal' and 'the Disloyal', so central to Arthur's approach, was dismissed. Rogers held that the claims about the unjust treatment of the minority in the proposals were without warrant, that the rebellious element in the majority was exaggerated, and that the scenario involving an inevitable break-up of the Union, if the Bill were implemented, was contrary to the terms contained within the Bill.[39] To him, Gladstone's proposals were 'bold and courageous', and merited widespread support.[40]

Rogers perceived Home Rule differently from Arthur because his starting point was fundamentally different. Denying that a separatist or anti-Union intention lay behind Gladstone's Bill, he insisted that the only union which could endure was one entered upon willingly in which there was an acceptable element of self-government.[41] The arbitrariness with which the Union had been established, and the absence of a degree of self-government, ensured its non-acceptability to the majority of people in Ireland. By satisfying 'the legitimate aspirations of the Irish people' for limited independence, Rogers argued, Home Rule would provide the only true safeguard for the Protestant minority. There was otherwise a fatal weakness in the stance of loyalists:

> They are entitled to the same protection as any other class of fellow-subjects; but they are taking an unfortunate position

when they declare that their safety depends upon the maintenance of a form of Government obnoxious to the majority of
the nation of which they are a part.[42]

Rogers dismissed what he described as 'brag and bluster'[43]
on the loyalist side, singling Orangeism out for special attack.
Turning to a prominent Orangeman, Mr de Cobain, a Member
of Parliament, described by a sympathiser as 'a devout man of
Wesleyan origin', Rogers quoted a published interview in which
de Cobain denied moral authority to Gladstone's government. If
need be, de Cobain claimed, Ulstermen would resort to arms to
defend their constitutional position.[44] Here, said Rogers, was a
form of loyalty similar to that shown by the Southern States to
the Union in America, a loyalty which consisted in devotion to a
government only in so far as that government acted in its sectional
interests.

True Protestantism, in contrast to Orangeism, had been cradled
in liberty, argued Rogers:

> Its life-blood is the breath of liberty, its true strength lies in
> the fullest exercise of liberty. But, alas! there have been too
> many Protestants who have not understood this ... A
> demand that four millions of Roman Catholics shall be
> deprived of a Constitution which would otherwise be
> accorded to them, and kept under the domination of thirty
> millions of Protestants, for the sake of the Protestant minority
> in their own country, is certainly difficult to reconcile with
> impartial justice to all creeds and all churches.[45]

While acknowledging that there was a persecuting tendency
within Roman Catholicism, exercised particularly through the
priesthood, Rogers denied that priests would exercise a controlling political influence in the event of Home Rule.[46] If, however,
oppressive measures were proposed by an administration in
Dublin, they could be blocked by the Lord Lieutenant within
Ireland or by the Imperial Parliament. Trust needed to be exercised
at this and other points. In any case Irish Protestantism must not
depend upon coercive legislation, nor could justice be denied to
a majority in Ireland for the sake of a minority.[47]

A century later there is an uncomfortably familiar ring about the arguments on both sides. Arthur's writings on Home Rule can still be consulted with profit, providing a clear and eloquent expression of Protestant fears, convictions and aspirations in the late nineteenth century. His discouragement of violence and recognition that care must be exercised in not identifying the churches officially with party politics, still have validity. Some will feel that by his own standards, he over-stepped the mark of acceptability in the vehemence of his opposition to Home Rule. He lacked the sensitivity to see and feel things from the point of view of the other main tradition. His view of Parnell, for example, was wholly negative, failing to take account of the competing claims of violent nationalism and constitutionalism with which Parnell struggled.[48] It could be argued that greater political astuteness on the part of unionists at that time could have enabled them to play a significant part in helping nationalists to resolve this crucial issue in ways more acceptable to unionist opinion and conducive to an acceptable political solution. The fault, however, did not lie only on one side. Nationalists did not define nationalism in a way that made it easy for the majority of Protestants to identify with it, nor did they provide much evidence that they understood or took seriously Protestant and unionist fears. Like many people in Ireland, Arthur was a product and prisoner of his past. He interpreted the Irish situation solely from a unionist standpoint, and refused to acknowledge that the union needed to be re-negotiated. In contrast to Parnell who maintained that Ireland was no mere geographical appendage of Britain, Arthur fervently believed that Ireland had been placed by God under Britain's protection. To him this was as much a matter of faith as of politics.

8

Apologist

William Arthur's contribution 'as an apologist grappling with the intellectual issues of his time' was, in the view of a recent writer, 'of major importance'.[1] Arthur's efforts in this field were mainly four publications: *On the Difference between Physical and Moral Law* (1883), *Religion without God* and *God without Religion* (published initially in parts from 1885), and *On Time and Space, Two Witnesses for a Creator* (1887). Given that the philosophical ideologies discussed by Arthur – positivism, agnosticism and deism – have passed through various stages and remain with us in different forms, it is worth examining Arthur's arguments. There are, however, difficulties. His style in places is now dated, and some of the authorities and particular issues he discussed are unfamiliar today.

Arthur first became aware of Auguste Comte (1798–1857), the French philosopher and founder of positivism, around 1843.[2] Comte's *Course of Positive Philosophy* was published in several volumes between 1830 and 1842. Although it was not translated into English for a decade, Arthur had the advantage of being appointed to France in 1846 and reading Comte in the original. Residence in Paris in 1847 and 1848, where Comte lived, would have sharpened his interest which continued over the years, Arthur noting variations as they developed under Comte and others. In the early 1860s he produced some notes on the subject, and was urged to expand and publish them.[3] This, however, he declined to do, for lack of time and in recognition of a need to develop his understanding of the issues involved. Eventually, as a consequence of deteriorating health and an inability to attend to other things, he took the opportunity to develop his thoughts on philosophical subjects through the late 1870s and the 1880s.

Comte affirmed that all knowledge regarding matters of fact

was based upon the 'positive' or scientific data of observation and experience, to which the inquirer must adhere strictly. Beyond the realm of fact there was a formal realm, that of pure logic and mathematics, concerned with 'the relations of ideas' which came to be classified as sciences. All allegedly transcendent knowledge – of metaphysics, theology and uncritical speculation – must be repudiated if it went radically beyond any possible evidence that could either support or refute it. At best theological language could not be considered more than the expression of human imagination. Positivism tended in a secular, anti-theological and anti-metaphysical direction, holding that for scientific purposes 'God' was an unnecessary assumption. Later the Logical Positivists were to take the further step of dismissing theological statements as meaningless.

Comte also devised an evolutionary scheme of intellectual development which he believed was paralleled in the evolution of thought patterns throughout human history and in the history of an individual's development from infancy to adulthood. This regarded thought in every field as passing progressively through three phases from superstition to science, by first being religious or theological; then metaphysical, with explanations being more abstract; and finally positivistic or scientific. In an attempt to fill the void left by what he regarded as the inevitable waning of Christian belief, Comte constructed a short-lived 'religion of humanity', with a ritual, a calendar, a priesthood (of scientists), and secular saints such as Julius Caesar, Dante and Joan of Arc. The English philosopher Herbert Spencer (1820–1903) presented a form of positivism in which religion was given a place beside science with reference to the unknown and unknowable Absolute. Comte also included a proposal for global social and political reforms. It is easy to dismiss his blueprint for future society as grandiose and even absurd, especially with the hindsight of over a century of subsequent history, but the reasoning behind his proposals cannot be so easily dismissed and the basic approach of his work has survived in a modified form in the Logical Positivism which has had such an influence in the twentieth century.

The central thesis of Arthur's *On the Difference between Physical and Moral Law* is that, despite some similarities, there are two fundamentally different kinds of law, physical law and moral law. On the basis of this thesis Arthur mounted an attack on positivism and presented an argument for the existence of God. The positivist doctrine was described by reference to a statement by John Stuart Mill, that it was Comte's view that 'all phenomena, without exception, are governed by invariable laws, with which no volitions, either natural or supernatural, interfere'.[4] Arthur took this to mean that minds and bodies were governed by laws of the same order, and a large part of his book was directed towards refuting that proposition. He implied that bodies, and material objects generally, were governed by physical laws, whereas minds were governed by moral laws. He then proceeded to argue that physical law and moral law were very different, though they did have in common that each determined a relation between one agent and other agents. In a lengthy discussion the two most important points were, first, that whereas a moral law could be disobeyed, the concept of disobedience did not apply to a physical law. The moral agent, though unable to break physical law, was able to break moral law; and the physical agent was not able to break any law, physical or moral. Also, the relations established by the two orders of laws differed in numerous ways. Among the heavenly bodies, for example, there were relations of illumination and reflection, and of magnitude, number, velocity and distance. None of these, however, involved any kind of moral obligation or any of the emotions that arose in connection with relations established by moral law.

The distinction on which Arthur was insisting was clearly valid. What is questionable, however, is its relevance to the main point at issue. A follower of Comte could accept the distinction between physical and moral law and still maintain that, whether or not human beings were subject to moral law, the phenomena of human behaviour were governed by the same sort of laws as physical phenomena. Comte indeed believed that even when theology and metaphysics had been banished, in accordance with his law of three phases, there would still be moral rules and laws of conduct. He evidently did not regard this as inconsistent in any way with his fundamental doctrine that human behaviour, individual and social, was governed by the laws of what he sometimes called 'social physics'. It can be seen therefore that acceptance of Arthur's distinction between physical and moral law, even when combined with the view that human beings are subject to moral law, does not directly lead to the overthrow of Comte's view. It does, however, highlight fundamental questions concerning it, and as the debate on these and other issues is taken further, Arthur's arguments have a part to play in the rejection of Comte's position.

Recognition of the two orders of laws and of their distinctive features had an additional role in Arthur's thinking, making an essential contribution to his version of the well-known argument from design which he fully expounded in the later part of his book. His view was that the combination of the two orders was a system of free agents and fixed instruments, in which the free agents had the power to modify phenomena so as to produce results. Because of the uniformity and inflexibility of physical laws, these results were calculable and predictable. Such a system, Arthur argued, presupposed an arranging and determining will whom we call 'God'. The argument from design was one to which he returned in later writings.

Arthur revealed himself in the book as a master of the argument ad absurdum, using hypothetical cases to expose the weaknesses of his academic opponents. A good example is where he likened the positivist objection that one could not see any 'ordering mind' to the argument of the French physician who claimed that he was a republican since, after performing many autopsies on both noble men and commoners, he had failed to find any difference between them! Arthur's comment was that even if a doctor had dissected many heart specialists and dentists and had found no difference between them, this would not weigh heavily with him when confronted by a case of bad teeth or of heart disease. He would know to which specialist he should refer each case.[5]

There is an interesting discussion on prayer and miracles in which Arthur considered man's power to modify phenomena. His definition of a miracle was an event which is marvellous to an inferior being but perfectly ordinary to a superior being. He likewise argued that prayer was not a request to suspend the laws of nature but to apply them, just as we use physical laws to turn waste ground into arable land. This kind of argument has been formulated by other people, but not often with the clarity and logical force which Arthur displayed.

In *Religion without God* and *God without Religion*, Arthur further considered positivism, agnosticism and deism as interpreted by Comte, Frederic Harrison, Herbert Spencer and Fitzjames Stephen. There is an important passage in his discussion of Comte when Arthur, to show the inadequacy of reducing any science to the observation of phenomena and laws, used the illustration of perceiving a mail coach.[6] When one sees a mail coach, one is to note its appearance, length, breadth, height, colour and so forth. One will also, however, search for its 'law' – eight miles an hour, or nine, or ten. But this is to treat the coach itself as a basic phenomenon, whereas the positivist would maintain that the idea of a coach is something which is built up from much more basic sense data. The same goes for the 'law' of the coach. Positivists would understand laws as the invariable regularities which accompany basic perceptions, thus allowing us to derive the more complex notions of material objects like mail coaches and everything else that goes with them. Arthur appears not to have grasped this, and therefore, much of his argument at this point would seem to be based on a mistaken view.

In a similar way Arthur argued that positivists and philosophical agnostics were part of 'the movement in retreat of Atheism'.[7] He also wanted to show that Comte's position amounted to the denial that God existed. He failed to appreciate that the positivist position was more threatening if it succeeded in showing that the assertion that God exists did not make sense. It may be that some of his contemporaries found the idea that the question of God is logically incapable of resolution a more hopeful development than the outright denial that he exists. The outcome of such a line of argument, however, may be to render theology even less relevant than speculation about life on another galaxy. The positivist could argue that although, for example, the question of life on another galaxy is incapable of resolution, it is at least possible to understand the idea since the concept of life on this planet is based on experience. According to the positivist's understanding, however, God has no basis in experience.

It is questionable whether Arthur grasped the true role which Comte envisaged for religion in his reorganized world. Having been forced to the conclusion that religious responses were an inevitable part of human interaction with the world, Comte proposed that religion should be used as a means of social control. Its importance was therefore seen to lie in its utilitarian value, rather than in its focus on 'God'. Perhaps a modern way of assessment might be in terms of the creation of myths and rituals, in order to convey a system of morality and social solidarity. To accuse such a 'religion' of failing to carry out many of the functions of Christianity would be to miss the point. One possible development of positivism would be for human beings to outgrow religion. If that were the case, its usefulness would simply disappear.

Arthur entered into historical and social arguments about the origin of religion and the probability of its survival. A large part of his writing attempted to demonstrate that the absence of religion would have undesirable social and moral consequences. Without a Christian basis, he argued, much of morality and civilized behaviour would disappear.[8] Such disputes are still with us.

Arthur was not fearful of Darwin. For example, he discussed the evolutionary theory of Ernst Haeckel, a zoologist and proponent of Darwinism, who popularized the theory of descent, and in whose monist philosophy the whole of nature was regarded as a unity and the concepts of design and a creator were rejected. Arthur insisted that the existence and creative activity of God had not been disproved:

> Were Haeckel's view true – were human life a mere blossom of animal life, animal life a mere branch of vegetable life, and vegetable life a mere effervescence of mineral existence – even that would not settle the question, and prove that there is no God. It might remain that an Almighty Being had commanded the waters and the earth to bring forth in a sense which would cover all the effects, and yet leave as the cause of those effects a living Maker.[9]

Arthur's comments on the early development of evolutionary theory were hampered by his inevitable ignorance of modern theories on the origins of simple life forms and modern genetic theory. Thus he argued from difficulties in current theories of spontaneous generation to the conclusion that we require a divine explanation to account for the link between the inanimate and the living. He noted the accepted orthodoxy that the human egg-cell in its form and constitution was not essentially different from those of other animals, and argued that the difference could only be accounted for by invoking the agency of God. This, of course, would now be regarded as an example of the unsatisfactory 'God of the gaps' type of reasoning.

The pamphlet *On Time and Space, Two Witnesses for a Creator* presented another version of the argument from design. Closely reasoned, it well illustrates Arthur's considerable capacity for analysing complex arguments. Philosophers of that time took great interest in the concepts of time and space, and wrote accounts of them which are somewhat puzzling to readers today. Some philosophers followed Immanuel Kant, foremost among the thinkers of the Enlightenment, in regarding time and space only as interpretative categories of the mind, with no necessary reference to anything in the outside world. In the greater part of his pamphlet, leading up to the argument from design, Arthur insisted that time and space were real entities, and listed a number of their distinctive features. When, for example, we question our consciousness we learn that it is possible to conceive of the absence from space of anything in it, such as the moon or the stars, or our earth from the universe. What we cannot conceive, however, is no Space. Similarly the mind can conceive the absence or non-occurrence of any event in time, but it cannot conceive of no Time. Time and Space are persistent. They depend on nothing, and while they have relation to everything, they remain, should everything cease to be. Time and Space are the medium through which we look from the world of bodies into that of infinite and eternal spirit, from things which are made, moved and governed, to that which designs, creates and orders things in their courses.

Time and Space have their instructive correspondences, continued Arthur. Time has three tenses – past, present and future – yet Time itself is one. Space has three dimensions – height, length and depth – yet Space too is one. There is no duration outside these categories of time, no dimension outside height, length and depth. Time and Space therefore point not only to deity, but also hint at trinity.

Arthur showed a good acquaintance with the literature on the subject, citing, among others, Lucretius, Locke, Kant and Sir William Hamilton. His espousal of the argument from design would, however, have been even more effective had he taken account of, and been able to reply to, criticisms that had been made of it, notably by Hume. The thesis Arthur advanced was that the structure of the universe was the result of interspaces (intervals between objects in space) and of intervals between events in time. Such a structure, it was claimed, must be the work of an intelligent creator. The analogy of the printer's types was effectively used:

> The printer's types are an apt illustration of the atoms; and to conceive of the types as originally so many pieces of shapeless metal, clashing themselves first of all into *a*, *b*, *c*, and *d*, as a preparation for other performances, exceeds surely the self-command even of a materialist ... Let him look at each letter, and then say if, in every case, the conjunction of inter-space with body is not structural, and if structure does not point back to proportion, proportion to design, and design to an intelligent agent.[10]

Arthur's philosophical writings are a monument to an except-ionally able man who was well in tune with the thinking of his day. He was an enthusiastic controversialist in the cause of theism and against positivism, and was sometimes excessively scornful of his opponents. He was well-informed with a particularly impressive range of scientific knowledge of which he made skilful use. His arguments were clearly expressed, his terms well defined. By studying Comte in the original French editions rather than through 'laudatory representations' or 'condensed and expur-gated' versions[11] compiled by English followers, he had an advan-tage in coming to grips with his thinking. He believed that Comte's powers as a thinker had been 'ridiculously exaggerated', and wrote of his 'ponderous and labyrinthian speculations'.[12] In discussing the theory that thought in every field passes through three phases, Arthur denied that the three states were universal, necessary, successive, or mutually exclusive.[13]

Arthur certainly possessed philosophical acumen and ability, though it cannot be said there was anything philosophically original in his writings. The success of his apologetics is a matter of opinion. Ways of thinking are often better understood from the perspective of time, when central issues can be more clearly seen, but in Arthur's writings we have a valiant and resourceful attempt to stand up for traditional Christianity, and to refute the arguments of its Victorian opponents. He thus presents a challenge to those in every age who assume that a simple gospel can be proclaimed without taking account of contemporary questions and doubts. Nothing can absolve each generation from the need to produce its own apologetic, relevant to its time and place. Such an enterprise is not an intellectual distraction. As with Arthur, it is an aspect of mission, part of an attempt to relate the gospel to every aspect of life.

9

William Arthur and Roman Catholicism

William Arthur was a convinced Methodist and a pan-evangelical. He opposed the raising of contentious, non-essential issues between churches especially when they threatened the church's credibility or impact on society. He encouraged co-operation between Christians and churches of like mind, affirming the link between union and mission. Methodism, he argued, had a special role to fulfil in the relation between churches. Its origin within the Church of England helped it to value catholicity and to avoid extremism. Its indebtedness in its own spirituality to a wide variety of Christian traditions made it aware of the need and opportunity to facilitate renewal in other churches.

Arthur, however, viewed high Anglicans and Roman Catholics differently. He believed that they had departed from the teaching of Christ and the New Testament, and he was particularly critical of the influence of their priests in such diverse fields as education, politics and mission. Arthur seldom numbered Catholics among his friends and acquaintances. It also has to be acknowledged that part of his motivation in pressing for evangelical co-operation was to facilitate resistance to Catholic influence. His opposition was never so strong, however, as to rule out the possibility of positive and creative encounter.

Arthur's stance on Catholicism was not unusual at that time. As David Hempton has made clear, John Wesley's attitude towards Catholicism was more ambivalent than has frequently been admitted. He viewed it as an essentially illiberal force, and in the generations following Wesley anti-Catholicism grew within Wesleyan Methodism.[1] British support for Methodism within Ireland was itself an expression of the attempt to resist Catholicism, and the flow of intelligence from Wesleyan missionaries who served in the Irish Mission contributed to a hardening of attitudes.

Catholicism came to be regarded as the primary cause of poverty in Ireland, being seen as an enemy of enlightened values and economic progress. The antidote to Catholicism was therefore seen to be evangelical conversion. Catholicism was viewed as 'all pervasive in influence, monolithic in scope, imperialist in intention, persecuting in its essential nature, and impoverishing in its social effects'.[2] This is the background to the opposition from Irish Methodists and others to a series of proposals relating to Catholics, including Catholic emancipation, attempts to repeal the Union between Britain and Ireland, the grant to Maynooth college, and the disestablishment of the Church of Ireland. The latter was interpreted as a weakening of the bulwark against Irish Catholicism. This all reflects a power struggle between fundamentally opposing world-views. Gladstone himself warned in his pamphlets on the Vatican in the mid–1870s, that Catholics loyal to their church would put allegiance to the Pope before duty to the Crown.

The position among British Nonconformists in the second half of the nineteenth century has been summarized:

> Anti-Catholicism had put down deep roots in Nonconformity. Roman Catholicism was seen as a rival faith, a perverted system of doctrine that misled souls about the way of salvation. Catholicism seemed to stand condemned by scripture ... Catholicism seemed utterly illiberal. The Catholic Church, it was supposed, was prepared to use power unscrupulously to impose its beliefs on others.[3]

Viewed in this light, Arthur's opinion that Protestantism and Catholicism were so fundamentally different as to be separate and opposed religions, can be better understood.

Non-theological factors often came into play in Protestant/ Roman Catholic relationships in Ireland. One example is the fear, felt by many Protestants, of the role of Catholic priests in Irish politics. Opinions differ as to the nature and scale of this, but it does appear that priests played an increasing part in political life as the century progressed. For example, in the campaign for Catholic emancipation from 1824 to 1829, priests often acted as local agents and organizers for the Catholic Association. They addressed public meetings, provided leadership in local committees and canvassed voters. To an extent, a high profile in such activities was inevitable, given the better education of priests and their standing in the community. Priests also became involved in the movement against the payment of tithes in the 1830s; in the agitation for the repeal of the Act of Union launched in 1840; and in a succession of political movements in the second half of the century, from the independent Irish Party in the 1850s to the Anti-Parnellite Nationalists in the 1890s. Between 1853 and 1892, nine Irish Members of Parliament were unseated on the grounds that their election had involved the exercise of undue influence by priests.[4]

Arthur's attitude towards Catholics was undoubtedly coloured by personal knowledge of community violence. Relatives and neighbours had suffered in shooting and other incidents in earlier periods of Irish history and within his own lifetime.[5] Such experiences undermined confidence, encouraged mistrust, impaired relationships and discouraged acceptance of radical political proposals such as Home Rule. These were undoubtedly factors in the opposition to Gladstone's proposals on the part of many Protestants and unionists. They had lived through the Fenian agitations, and could recall violent expressions of the land struggle, including evictions, boycotts and killings. Fear of 'the lawless Irish' increased, and led to a resolve to resort, if necessary, to force in defence of the Union. Arthur, however, resisted this development, believing that violence would be counter-productive.

Arthur's espousal of the predominantly Protestant loyalist cause, together with his rejection of the mainly Catholic nationalist cause, reflected both political and spiritual conviction. In his understanding, the sovereign rights of Christ over Ireland, exercised through enlightened Protestant British rule, were at stake. 'My native country is to be pushed off from the elder sister, under whose wing the Creator has placed her', he complained concerning Home Rule.[6] This accounts for the heightened sense of betrayal which Arthur and many loyalists felt when Gladstone formed an alliance with Parnell. In their view Gladstone was putting morality and religion at risk for highly questionable political gain. Any suggestion that the granting of a measure of self-government could be justified in terms of justice for Ireland, or that it was the product of enlightened Christian concern for Ireland, was wholly rejected. T.F. Shillington, a prominent Irish Wesleyan layman and Liberal, expressed the case against Home Rule forcefully in 1892:

> The Home Rule scheme proposed we reject *in toto* . . . It would terribly aggravate the existing differences between Protestant and Roman Catholic . . . I have no sympathy with the 'No Popery' cry. I long to see the time when the memories of past differences on all sides will be provided with decent Christian burial, but I detest with all my heart the idea of clerical domination, the spiritual guide assuming control in both spiritual and temporal affairs . . . There is an aversion to Home Rule in the North of Ireland deep-rooted far beyond the belief of those who are lightly playing with this question. With thousands of good men it exists with all the intensity of an article of faith which it is dangerous to trifle with.[7]

Home Rule posed a threat to British imperialism which, interpreted as trusteeship, was regarded as a legitimate manner in which Britain could influence other countries for good and for God. Political concessions, such as Gladstone had in mind for Ireland, would on the other hand damage the British Empire as a whole, according to Arthur, sowing the seeds of disintegration in the minds of politicians and others so that countries such as India would be affected. The choice for many, writes Hempton, was 'between Imperial Protestant glory and a tyrannical impoverished Catholic state'.[8]

Accepting the vigour of Arthur's opposition to Catholicism, the integrity with which he studied developments in Catholic belief and practice over many years remains impressive. It necessitated visits to libraries in different countries to study original materials and to meet scholars. His investment of time in this connection was enormous. He took no short-cuts, and appears to have spared no expense. He does not seem to have consulted prejudiced, polemical material from Protestant or other sources, nor did he resort to superficial summaries of the issues. Instead he drew on official documents and histories, approved journals and periodicals, contemporary books and pamphlets, including those written both from an Ultramontanist and a liberal Catholic view-point.

Arthur's grasp of the Italian, French and German languages – 'his extraordinary gift of tongues'[9] – stood him in good stead, as did the contacts he established with diplomats, politicians and scholars. Among the latter, his personal acquaintance with Dr Döllinger, the distinguished Catholic liberal historian, was especially helpful, giving him access to important collections of material. Arthur's criticisms of Roman Catholicism were therefore his own, carefully thought out and based on wide reading. He quoted extensively from Catholic sources, and although his quotations were of necessity selective they were also accurate.

The pontificate of Piux IX (Pio Nono) from 1846 to 1878, which is the longest in history, was momentous for Catholicism. Pius early introduced a series of modest reforms in an attempt to win popular support for the papacy. This followed criticism by Italian nationalists of Austrian influence in the Italian peninsula, and pressures from liberals within the church for change. The reforms, however, proved to be a case of 'too little, too late', and were followed by a succession of political reverses over more than two decades. These left the Pope a virtual prisoner within the Vatican. Main features in the pontificate included the loss of control over the papal states, the dogma of the Immaculate Conception, the Syllabus of Errors, the convening of the first Vatican Council and the doctrine of Papal Infallibility. Attacks on liberalism and the enunciation of conservative dogmas reflect the Pope's disappointment that his early reforms had failed to strengthen his position. He became convinced that spiritual power could only be protected by the exercise of temporal power.

Arthur commented on Ultramontanism in an article in 1853, directing attention to the contrast between the Pope's political losses and his claims to power. Ultramontanism, literally meaning 'beyond the mountains', indicates a strong emphasis on papal authority and centralization within the church by those who look beyond the Alps for guidance, that is, to the Pope. Yet the Pope, claimed Arthur:

> wearing the triple tiara to typify his supremacy, maintains his seat only by favour of French protection and Austrian bayonets; the dispenser of power cannot negotiate even the

most beggarly loans; and the tiara itself, if put up for sale, would scarcely fetch the price of its own gewgaws. But the pretensions of Rome have always been in the direct ratio of its decrepitude; its usurpations have been the most arrogant and progressive, when its legitimate authority in its own circumscribed territory was most in question. It is so now. Pius IX sits upon a tottering chair, and yet he is giving laws to Europe.[10]

Ultramontanism, argued Arthur, was a single-minded attempt to restore the philosophy, policies and practices of the mediaeval period.

Despite the radical differences between Protestants and Roman Catholics, Arthur recognized that at the personal level Protestants, without compromising their reformed and biblical position, had to be fair and positive towards Catholics. In *Italy in Transition* (1860), having observed the Pope in Rome during Holy Week, he described him as 'a very fine old man' whose face beamed 'with apparently true benignity'. He seemed to be 'a noble old man . . . very kind and sincere'.[11] In conversation with a coachman, also in Rome, who was fiercely critical of the Catholic Church, Arthur suggested that there were many good priests. The coachman was unimpressed, however, and dismissed Arthur as 'rather milk and water, for not hating the Priests more'.[12] Arthur attended services in various towns and cities, and commented that in contrast to what he had found in Protestant worship in France, Switzerland and Italy, the singing in some German and Italian Catholic churches came 'as near to my idea of what Christian singing ought to be, as to its composition and style, as anything I have heard'.[13] He described a Capuchin preacher in Bologna as honest and gifted, though fundamentally mistaken in his beliefs.[14] In Rome he gave no encouragement to those who were inclined to talk about moral scandals in the Vatican. 'Impurity leaves a soil everywhere', he observed.[15] Later, in his introduction to *Count Campello* (1881), the autobiography of a nobleman and priest who had been converted and left the Catholic Church, Arthur welcomed the fact that the converted priests whom he knew personally did not dwell on negative points such as the corruption surrounding celibacy. Instead they properly and positively emphasized the reality of God's redeeming grace through Christ. Of Campello himself, Arthur commented that his mind was on too high a plain 'to rake among the rubbish'.[16]

Arthur also discussed the Roman Catholic Church's prospects of reform, in *Italy in Transition*, and had an open mind on the subject. He quoted one person, 'apparently conversant with public questions' in Italy, as favouring the view that the church would be reformed and that all Christians in Italy would become one in essentials.[17] Arthur himself confessed that he did not feel competent to assess 'how far the minds of thinkers and public men' generally were 'turned to the probability of a national reform'. Some people 'who ought to know the Priests well', he noted, were confident that large numbers of them were eager for reform. His own impression of politicians, however, was that in general they had not yet dared to consider the question seriously. They displayed a pragmatic approach to the church, meeting each difficulty as it arose. Understandably, they were content at present to make steady progress in securing political liberties, leaving questions relating to the church to another day. The lines of communication should therefore be kept open, Arthur believed, and Roman Catholicism should be studied with integrity and objectivity. Possibly Catholics could still be recalled to the essentials of the Christian faith. Prominent among these were obedience to Christ and faithfulness to the traditions of the Apostles and of the primitive church, as indicated in the New Testament.

The pace against reform quickened, however. In 1864, the Syllabus of Errors was issued. It listed and condemned what were regarded as eighty of the principal 'errors' of the time, including pantheism, socialism, civil marriage, secular education and religious indifferentism. The Syllabus made public what had earlier been proclaimed to and among the bishops, and made general earlier denunciations of particular events. The eightieth article stigmatized as an error the view that the Pope 'can and should reconcile himself to and agree with progress, liberalism, and modern civilization'. The issuing of the Syllabus dealt a severe blow to liberal and reforming elements within the church.

A year later Arthur still believed that political developments in other parts of Italy could exercise a liberalizing influence on the Vatican:

There is good reason to hope that the national religion will be purified from much of its superstition; and that while some of its gorgeous services may still be cherished by the 'objective' minded Italians, its priests will no longer be able to enslave and terrify, nor pervert the glorious liberty of the Gospel into the engine of despotism. No sooner was Milan freed ... than the Scriptures in the vernacular were openly sold beneath the very shadow of the cathedral ... Neither Austria nor the Papacy can resist the influences which beset them on every side.[18]

The convening of the first Vatican Council in late 1869, with its decisions in 1870, radically undermined the position of liberal Catholics and signified the triumph of the conservative party within the church. Arthur described in considerable detail the colourful, opening ceremony at the Vatican Council, which he considered inappropriate from a Christian point of view. It seemed, however, to prefigure for Catholics the glorification, almost the deification, of the Pope.[19] Highlighting the differences of opinion among participants at the Vatican Council, Arthur drew attention to the procedures adopted to thwart and silence those who opposed the Curia's policies. Important permanent committees, including that on dogma, were packed with 'Infallibilist' members, and the time allocated for study and comment on draft documents was deliberately reduced.[20] This corresponded, claimed Arthur, with a process whereby, in the years preceding the convening of the Vatican Council, the triumph of Ultramontanism had been assured. Within the Council itself, theologians were marginalized, petitions ignored, some critics were not invited to speak, and those who were given an opportunity to voice their opposition received little coverage in official reports. To lessen controversy and avoid the divisiveness of a vote, there was an unsuccessful attempt to pass the dogma on Infallibility by acclamation. Some liberals left the Council early, feeling impotent to influence the course of events.[21] Among those who remained, Döllinger offered some of the sharpest comments. Arthur's summary of what he said is worth noting:

The Church he had toiled to rehabilitate before the intellect of the Fatherland, striving, by letters, to connect her more firmly with the past, and to equip her more nobly for the future, had been cast into the cauldron. The very basis of dogma was to be changed. What his teachers had taught him, what he for nearly half a century had been teaching his pupils as the indispensable test of additional dogmas, was now to be dispensed with, and a new standard was to be set up, which he had learnt and taught, was not of authority. The adoption of that standard would change the relation of the Church to the Bible and to the Fathers, to General Councils, and to the Episcopate, to the people and the king, to letters and all lights, to liberties, constitutions, and every human hope. Principles which had been charged upon them by Protestants, and which they had resented ... were now lifting their heads in a General Council ... The Infallibilists were the Pope, the Curia, the Jesuits, and the majority of the bishops ... The cold hand of absolution, thrice absolute, (was) closing in like a vice upon the Church, compressing her into a sect shut up within the will of a single person.[22]

The decisive vote on the dogma of Infallibility was taken on 13 July 1870, and was carried by an overwhelming majority. Four hundred and fifty-one voted for it, eighty-eight against it, and sixty-two in favour of some amendment. Arthur expressed regret and concern at the manner in which opposition had been eroded in the course of the Council, believing that it augured ill for the church in the future. He regarded the insertion of an additional phrase in the final stages of consideration, *non autem ex consensu ecclesiae*, as being particularly serious, since it denied to the church through the bishops any role in defining doctrine and morals:

> Done in a moment! the Romish bishops had effaced from their law, and from their rule of faith the consent of the Catholic Church! Talk of revolutions, of hasty parliamentary votes, of the sudden impulse of a mob; but where in history is there an instance of breaking with a long and loud-resounding past, in such haste, and so irrevocably ...? It is for the unborn to judge the men who did that act and then faced round, saying that they had changed nothing.[23]

Arthur's assessment of the implications of the Council's decisions make sombre reading, for Catholics and non-Catholics alike. He did not question the right of the Catholic Church to define its doctrines, nor the right of individual Catholics to practise their religion, except where such doctrine and practice interfered with the rights of others. *The Pope, the Kings, and the People* (1877) contains his fullest thoughts on Pius' pontificate, and its sub-title provides a clue as to how he viewed developments, 'A History of the Movement to make the Pope Governor of the World by a Universal Reconstruction of Society'. His view of the role of Italian Jesuits between 1850 and 1870 had a wider application. They invested theological terms with political meanings, and set their sights on the complete social, political and religious reconstitution of the world, with the Pope as the acknowledged head of authority:

> They loudly proclaimed . . . the revocation of constitutions, the abolition of modern liberties, especially those of the Press and of worship, with the subjection to canon law of civil law, and, above all, the subjection to the jurisdiction of the Pope of all nations and their rulers.[24]

The Jesuits, claimed Arthur, had set themselves the task of reversing the process which had been set in motion by John Wycliffe in the fourteenth century:

> As he had striven for the emancipation of kings from the Pope, of legislatures from the ecclesiastical powers, and of the individual from the priest, so did they set themselves to bring back again the dominion of the priest over the individual, the dominion of the ecclesiastical authorities over lawgivers, and above all, the dominion of the Pope over kings . . . In all their writings society was taken as meaning, not families, nor Churches, but nations, and each one of the nations was to form a province within a Church ruling over it and over all other nations in every one of their laws and public institutions.[25]

Making the state subject to the church, with the Pope possessing the right to exercise lordship over the civil power, was the most ominous development according to Arthur. It would, he argued, have a sinister bearing on the nature and aims of Catholic participation in such areas as education, the press and elections.[26]

In this connection Arthur drew attention to a situation in Germany following the Vatican Council. As some bishops, priests and others refused to submit to the dogma of Papal Infallibility, and the Vatican urged excommunication, one German lawyer ruled that people who had been excommunicated could not function in the courts as judges, advocates, or witnesses. The Governments of Prussia and Bavaria, however, refused to take sides in the dispute, continuing to regard all Catholics as equal in the eyes of the law irrespective of their position on Infallibility.[27] The special role of the Catholic Church in the Republic of Ireland in the twentieth century, and the Irish Government's record on such issues as divorce, censorship and the treatment of minorities, have led many people to conclude that the fears identified by Arthur and others were well-founded.

Given that the differences between Protestants and Roman Catholics were so great, it is remarkable that an important public debate was allowed to take place in Rome in 1872, on St Peter's associations with the city. The Catholic tradition, contested by Protestants, is that Peter founded the Church in Rome, and was pontiff there for a long period. The debate was conducted in a formal, sensitive and dignified manner, with an equal number of speakers and chairmen supplied by each side. An invited audience of Protestants and Catholics was instructed not to display its feelings, and the participants were required to observe the conventions of 'gentlemanly' conduct, by shaking hands and not interrupting one another.[28] At the outset it was a Protestant convert, a former Catholic monk, who suggested that they open with prayer.[29] Arthur associated himself with the debate in that he translated the report for publication, from Italian into English.

The discussion inevitably focussed on the biblical evidence and its interpretation, and on the weight to be attached to historical tradition whether or not it had strong scriptural support. The presentation of the Protestant viewpoint appears to have been more lively, and although no vote was taken there was a feeling at the end that the Catholics had lost out in the debate. The event attracted attention in both the Italian and the British press, partly because it was assumed that the Vatican had given permission for the debate to take place. The correspondent in *The Times* plainly went too far when he speculated that perhaps intolerance was declining.[30] Concern at a high level that the Catholic point of view had not been presented well was reflected a month later, when a three-day religious festival was convened in St Peter's, Rome. According to *The Times*, its purpose was to offer reparation for 'the horrible blasphemies with which . . . infidels' had denied the presence of Peter in Rome.[31] Despite this negative reaction, and the differences between the two sides, the fact and manner of the debate suggests that the participants saw themselves as belonging to the same family of faith.

'Bigotry', declared John Wesley in a sermon on the theme, 'is too strong an attachment to, or fondness for, our own party, opinion, Church, and religion.'[32] From this standpoint, Arthur was no bigot. He was a committed Methodist, who for example believed that the 'no politics' tradition precluded Methodist ministers from appearing on political platforms, but he none the less denied that this rule had any relevance to others. They, as far as he was concerned, were free to act as they saw fit. In a similar way he staunchly upheld the Wesleyan tradition of independence from state control, but distanced himself from Nonconformists who attacked the different tradition of the established Church of England. Strong commitment to one's own position, combined with a recognition that others thought and acted differently, were to him key elements in Methodism. These, together with an affirmation of the centrality of Christ, pointed the only reliable way forward in Christian co-operation and inter-church relations. He saw the quest for uniformity as the enemy of unity. On one occasion, in conversation with the Bishop of Lincoln, he quoted, 'one Lord, one faith and one baptism', to which the bishop replied that St Cyprian had added 'one bishop'. Arthur's rejoinder was that breaches in unity had always been caused by 'St Somebody adding something'.[33] An address at the Wesleyan Methodist Conference, attended by ministers of various evangelical churches, provided Arthur with an opportunity to share his reflections on this theme:

> I can give a man credit when he is brought up in a narrow system, and becomes liberal; then he is better than his system;

but when a man is brought up in a liberal body, like Method-ism, and becomes narrow, he is worse than his system. We each have our own distinct organization, doctrine, and disci-pline. If, as Methodists, we possess advantages in our own peculiar position, we have also disadvantages. I never feel the slightest tendency to be impatient either with Dissenters or Churchmen who find fault with me because I do not think as they do. I always prefer to take my own course. I believe that man is best calculated to be catholic in sentiment and liberal towards others who adheres most firmly to his own views.[34]

Taking up a familiar topic, the inappropriateness of uniformity in the search for unity, he proceeded to affirm the need for Christians to be at one in essentials:

As the centre of the universe is not Jupiter, the largest planet, or Venus, the brightest, but the sun; so the centre of the Church . . . (is) not Christians, but Christ. I do not want to ask whether you or we are doing this or that particular work; I rather rejoice that we are all endeavouring to be faithful to Christ.[35]

Once, when addressing a group of Baptist pastors, Arthur heard some of them speaking unfavourably of C.H. Spurgeon, then a young man. Arthur expressed the hope that God would one day use Spurgeon for some great spiritual work, to which the reply came that he would think differently if he had heard Spurgeon denounce Methodist teaching. 'I do not care', Arthur responded, 'if he exalts my Master.'[36] The story well illustrates Arthur's position and is in line with the spirit of Methodism.

'Think not the bigotry of another is any excuse for your own,' Wesley cautioned. 'Let him have all the bigotry to himself,'[37] he added. The extent to which this spirit was not shown towards Catholicism is an indication of how far it was believed the Catholic Church had departed from the centrality of Christ and the scriptures. Arthur laid down his view of this in his famous lecture on the British Empire:

Protestants have distinctions; but they have not different religions. They acknowledge, alone, the Holy Trinity in unity, as the object of worship, and the canonical Scriptures as the standard of faith ... They have one faith, one hope, one baptism, one God and Father, one religion. But the Roman Catholic, having objects of worship to which the Protestant will not kneel, and standards of faith which he will not acknowledge; these two learn their doctrines from different sources, and offer their prayers to different beings; consequently, their religion is different.[38]

James Rigg acknowledged of Arthur that 'Roman Catholics ... were but exceptionally found in his family circle, nor were Oxford Ritualists' often in his company.[39] Arthur deeply feared the outcome of the Vatican Council, as did many others. Ultramontanism, suggests a writer recently, was 'distinguished by its political conservatism, its exaltation of papal authority, and its acceptance of a dogmatic, combative theology'.[40] In the light of the Council's decisions, Arthur declared, Roman Catholicism bore the word 'irreformable' self-inscribed on its forehead. Yet in 1891, he publicly welcomed the fact that in the second Methodist Ecumenical Conference there had been no denunciation of Roman Catholicism, nor a panic claim that 'Romanism was sweeping the earth'.[41] Sustained and sensitive contacts and evangelism were, by implication, still required. As ever, the mission of Christ remained paramount.

10

The Man and his Message

Nineteenth-century proprieties, William Arthur's own reticence, and the lack of relevant material from sources other than Arthur himself, make it impossible to fill in every detail of his life. Little is known, for example, of the role of his father within the family, and there are differences of opinion as to how many children were born to William and his wife.[1] Allowances have to be made for this when interest is aroused, and further information is sought.

His Appearance

What did Arthur look like? There are several striking portraits of him in his later years. He is balding, with deep set eyes. The corners of his mouth are upturned and he looks a kind, good-humoured man. Earlier references suggest that he never appeared robust, and that he had 'blue Celtic eyes' and 'a tinge of red' in his hair.[2] On his return from India after the breakdown in his health, his frail appearance was felt to be an asset when he was pleading the missionary cause. A detailed though rather flowery description of him was written in his presidential year when he was forty-seven:

> Slenderly, but proportionately built, with a small head, the part below the eyes almost diminutive, yet greatly expressive; above the eye is a beautifully bright, round, lofty, cranium, without an indentation or projection anywhere.[3]

His Relationships

Arthur discloses very little about his relationship with his parents and siblings. There is a suggestion that, at least initially, his parents disapproved of his first association with the Methodists and his early preaching.[4] When he left for India in 1839, his mother's identification with him was therefore important to him. 'From the Lord I received thee, and to the Lord I give thee up,' he reported her as saying.[5] His next meeting with her, however, was not till 1855 in America, where he found her in 'one of the sweetest spots in the world'.[6] One can only wonder why there was no meeting between them after his return from India in 1841, and prior to her departure for America probably in the middle to late 1840s. Did he visit Ireland at all in that period? If so, why did he not travel to Newport? His poor health and severe conditions in Ireland would have been inhibiting factors.

In his writings and public utterances, Arthur does not seem to have spoken of his father. In receiving news of his mother's death in 1855, Arthur reflected that 'perhaps no woman had ever suffered more in mind, body & estate'.[7] Was this a reference to the harsh effects of the famine in the west of Ireland, and perhaps a hint at some difficulty or disappointment in relation ⋅ ⋅ his father?

Arthur had two brothers, Lt. Colonel A.M. (Alec) Arthur of the 11th Devonshire Regiment, and James K. Arthur. The first was a director of the Star Life Assurance Society, which had Methodist associations.[8] James K. Arthur assisted William in translating material from Italian into English.[9] As already noted, the relationship William Arthur had with his sister and brother-in-law, Mr and Mrs James Lindsay, was particularly close.[10]

Little is known of the circumstances surrounding Arthur's marriage. He was to have married Sarah Jane Ogle of Leeds, the daughter of a well-to-do businessman, but in a letter to Rigg in October 1848 he commented that she had almost died of diabetes.[11] She died before the marriage took place, and Arthur married her sister Elizabeth Ellis Ogle in June 1850. Perhaps such arrangements were not unusual in those days.

Arthur's wife travelled with him when he went abroad for health reasons. In this connection he refused offers of help from the WMMS towards his travel expenses, preferring to meet them from his own resources.[12] When in Britain, his wife probably maintained the Methodist tradition for hospitality to a wide range of people. In the will of their daughter Agnes, who died in 1934, there is mention of 'one signature in red ink of the Rajah of Koorg (framed)' given to her mother after she had provided hospitality for him.[13] The Arthur's final home in Britain was a house on Clapham Common, formerly occupied by a Christian banker associated with William Wilberforce. It became a meeting place for prominent people in church and state. Arthur, however, was not one for name dropping, and little is known of their guests.

Arthur's wife took ill in 1885 and died in 1888, the year in which he retired. The marriage had produced five daughters, but no sons. The eldest died from typhoid during Arthur's period at Methodist College, Belfast.[14] Emily married Anderson Fowler, a prominent New York businessman whose family came from Co. Fermanagh, in the northern part of Ireland and they had fourteen children, of whom Arthur baptized ten. Lillie spent many years as companion to Lady Lycett, and died a few years after her mother. Mary and Agnes cared for their father until his death.

Arthur's friendship with James Rigg is the relationship on which most information is available, since many of their letters have been preserved and reproduced.[15] They first met in July 1845, when Arthur was on the staff at Wesley's Chapel, and Rigg was undergoing tests as a candidate for the Wesleyan ministry. In the interval for refreshments, as Arthur was 'distributing the buns', he surprised Rigg by greeting him by name and speaking warmly of Rigg's father whom he had recently met in Leeds.[16] A few days later Arthur came on missionary deputation to Bedfordshire and stayed with a farmer, Mr Samuel Bennett, where Rigg himself was already a guest. The two young men were thrown into each other's company and quickly became 'fast and intimate friends'.[17] Rigg's mother was Anne M'Mullen, the daughter of an Irish Wesleyan preacher who had been appointed to Gibraltar. At the age of seven she had accompanied her parents. Within a few days of their arrival they had all developed yellow fever, and Anne was the sole survivor. She was brought up in England in the family of Dr Adam Clarke, the renowned Wesleyan scholar. Perhaps Arthur and Rigg felt a bond in their Irish ancestry. Their common interest in India, and the fact that both had trouble with their eyes which hindered their work there, also drew them together. In Arthur's case it necessitated his return to Britain after less than two years. The oculist whom Rigg consulted about his eye problem had said that his sight would not 'allow him to labour under a tropical sun', so that although he was designated for India he never set foot in the country.[18]

The friendship between Arthur and Rigg was rich and mutually helpful. It was of the mind and spirit, and was nurtured largely through correspondence. In the spring of 1846, Rigg observed Arthur on missionary deputation in Cornwall, and greatly admired his straightforward style, intellectual vigour and spiritual power. He was particularly impressed by the fact that each talk was different and was delivered without notes, as were all Arthur's addresses. There may have been an element of hero worship on Rigg's part at the beginning, but the relationship quickly became one of mutual respect. Their correspondence reads as one between equals. They exchanged manuscripts and drafts of articles before publication, and valued each other's criticisms. Very early in their relationship Arthur wrote to Rigg:

> Accept my most unfeigned, most hearty thanks for your criticisms. To touch the good points is kind, to show the bad ones downright brotherly ... If you only continue similar strictures you will confer on me a favour not to be estimated; and as you go on you will hit harder.[19]

Their friendship was based on acceptance of one another and respect for truth as each perceived it, and was able to withstand the great strain placed on it in later years when they disagreed fundamentally on educational policy.

Glimpses of Arthur's disposition emerge in letters to Rigg. In October 1849, in response to Rigg's enquiry, Arthur wrote:

> I am happy – very happy – in my work and feel a persuasion, that does not falter, that God means to use me for His glory. My weak point is in private prayer. There I wander strangely. Often my thoughts are far more collected and upward when not upon my knees than when there. But in this also, by God's blessed mercy, I shall be conqueror.[20]

There is something rather touching in this confession of human weakness. His declaration of happiness and confidence in God's plan for him in spite of poor health is impressive.

As Arthur took up the position of President of Methodist

College, Belfast, in 1868, Rigg was appointed Principal of Westminster College on Arthur's proposal, a position he held until his retirement in 1903. Arthur's advice to his friend on this occasion was perhaps a reflection of Rigg's half-brother's impression of Arthur twenty years earlier, as a practical person as well as one of 'literary genius'.[21] 'May God go with you to Westminster!', Arthur wrote, adding, 'put on special care in the domestic department'.[22]

In his appreciation of Arthur in the *Methodist Recorder* of 14 March 1901, Rigg wrote:

> Sometimes, though rarely, in the following years we differed in judgment more or less seriously, but through the fifty-five years which have passed we never for a day lost each other's affection or suspended our confidential relations as friends and correspondents.[23]

This is a remarkable tribute to the close bond that existed between them.

His Health

Arthur's poor health put severe limitations on his ministry. It confined him to temperate climates, and restricted the amount of preaching, reading and writing he could do. It is a matter of speculation as to the difference it would have made to his life and work if he had been more robust.

The problem with his eyes, within months of his arrival in India, was a cruel blow to a young man who had looked forward so passionately to his missionary work, and who had started so enthusiastically. He sought the best medical advice, and tried a cooler climate, but it was all to no avail. On his return to Britain, after less than two years, he had to wear coloured spectacles and for a time was not allowed to read or write. This must have been a great disadvantage to him in the preparation of talks and sermons, but he quickly developed the mental powers that enabled him to deliver long talks and speeches without notes.

To add to his eye problems, he developed trouble with his throat, often complaining of hoarseness and at times loss of voice. His voice broke down in 1850, and while he had periods of remission it could not be relied upon. Often he could not speak above a whisper, and on occasions addresses by him had to be delivered by others. He also had problems with his chest. Many years after the event, he gave an account of how his illness had begun. He had addressed a 'ragged school' meeting in a crammed Exeter Hall in 1847. It had been a 'prodigious' event. It was raining when he left, and as he could not afford a cab he 'mounted on the knife-board of an omnibus'. He was 'worn down with overwork, preaching and speaking . . . and caught a chill . . . and (was) spitting blood'. This he described as his 'utter breakdown'.[24]

Ill health plagued him throughout his life. It was often necessary for him to be relieved of his responsibilities, and at times he sought improvement abroad, hoping that a change of scene and climate might aid a recovery. He also tried various treatments, but none had the desired effect. Even as late as 1897 he wrote to Rigg that he had had his throat 'burned with electricity'. More than thirty years earlier, he reflected, when being urged to try a new remedy, he had commented that he thought he had tried everything short of amputation![25] It is good to note that throughout his trials he retained his sense of humour.

Arthur did not disclose anything about the diagnosis of his illness. Tuberculosis reached its peak in Britain in the middle of the nineteenth century. The chill he caught in 1847 could have developed into pneumonia, which in turn may have led to tuberculosis. Tubercle bacillus in the sputum could also have affected the larynx and caused his hoarseness and frequent loss of voice. Such a diagnosis would explain why he was allowed to take long leaves of absence on the continent, as this was a recognized form of treatment for those who could afford it. The stigma surrounding tuberculosis would account for the lack of open reference to it.

Alternatively Arthur could have developed bronchiectasis from pneumonia. This could have led to persistent coughing and occasional blood-stained sputum such as Arthur mentioned. In this case, the hoarseness would have been unrelated and may have been caused by nodules forming on the vocal cords, such as speakers and singers sometimes develop. A diagnosis of sarcoidosis would also take account of the problems with his eyes, but since such a condition had not been identified in Arthur's life time, this is speculation.

His National Identity

Arthur was born and lived in Ireland prior to partition, a country which was part of the United Kingdom of Great Britain and Ireland. He was passionately pro-British and fiercely anti-Home Rule, and referred to himself in some circumstances as English. Others too thought of him as English on occasions, when, for example, they drew a distinction between Britain and America, or between 'Catholic Ireland' and 'Protestant Britain'. At other times, however, Arthur was not averse to using his Irish birth to his advantage. During his time in Paris, in the political upheavals of 1848, he was able to attend private political gatherings by passing as a sympathetic Irish patriot. 'Je suis Irlandais', he announced as he entered.[26] When J.C. Rigg, James Rigg's half-brother, first met Arthur in London in 1848, he referred to him as 'an Irishman'. Arthur himself once drew attention to the intriguing nature of his nationality. 'The oldest blood I can trace in my veins is Irish', he claimed, 'the next to that is English, and a good deal of it Scotch – so that I am mixed.'[27] Many Irish people will be able to identify with that statement, living in a situation made even more complex by the introduction of partition in 1921.

His Character

Arthur's reluctance to talk about his health is in some degree a reflection of the times in which he lived and of his general unwillingness to discuss bodily matters. There is an interesting example of this in his biography of Samuel Budgett, when he described the death of Budgett's son from cholera. The main and often the only symptom of cholera is violent diarrhoea, yet Arthur could only bring himself to write about 'cramp' and 'vital powers . . . sinking fast'.[28]

Similarly, little information is provided on Arthur's financial status. According to James Rigg there were two periods, neither of long duration, when Arthur was relatively well off.[29] Possibly these were after his marriage and following his sister's death.

There were other periods of relative poverty. One, already mentioned, was when he could not afford to hire a cab.[30] On another occasion he complained about having to pay a dollar to an American publishing house for a copy of one of his own books, at a time when he could ill afford it.[31] He appears, however, to have been content with his lot. In a letter written to Rigg before his marriage, when his future father-in-law had run into financial difficulties, he was thankful that Methodist ministers were not subject to such swings of fortune:

> We Methodist Preachers are a happy race. Poor though we be, how preferable is uniform poverty with wants and hopes proportioned to that fitful or at best uncertain affluence which inflates, vitiates, and departs, or if it stay, stays often to gild a cold and wooden heart.[32]

In an appreciation of Arthur, Rigg praised his generosity. Whether he was poor or rich, Rigg wrote, he was always an 'open-handed Christian Irishman'.[33] Apart from when something was to be gained from publicized donations, Arthur's giving was normally in secret.

There have been references to Arthur's saintliness. He had the capacity to make adjustments, and to maintain hope, dignity and usefulness in the face of broken health and frustrated plans. This is an aspect of saintliness. E.E. Jenkins, a former Indian missionary and WMMS Secretary, wrote of Arthur's 'inner sight', which he regarded as a vital part of his make-up.[34] By this he meant that Arthur tended to come to conclusions intuitively rather than through logic or reasoned argument. He viewed Arthur more as a seer than a formal theologian, one who beheld and sought to communicate visions. Those who came into contact with Arthur sometimes felt that a 'halo of sacredness' surrounded him, and were conscious of an 'indefinable reverence' in his presence.[35] Yet he was also described as 'full of fun and good humour'.[36] Self-effacing, he declined a doctorate from Dickinson College in 1856.[37]

Without doubt, Arthur was a man of principle. He knew his own mind, and was rarely prepared to alter his position or to compromise. There is abundant evidence of this in the stands he took, for example, over education, Roman Catholicism and Home

Rule. This must have made him a difficult person to relate to, and led to crises. In 1860, partly because of sharp policy differences with colleagues on Irish matters, he submitted his resignation as a WMMS Secretary. This, however, was withdrawn in 1861. His friendship with Rigg was put under severe strain over their differences on the education question. Although Arthur was adamant in standing up for his beliefs and principles, even when this meant opposing those who were more senior and perhaps more highly regarded than himself, he was able to do it with good grace and in such a way that he retained the loyalty of friends and the respect of those who opposed him. In his obituary of Arthur, John Telford paid particular attention to this aspect of his nature:

> He was one of the champions of progress and liberal policy in Conference ... He never lost his independence; never owned a master, yet never played the part of a rebel ... (He was) no partisan. Where there were failures or defects in public administration he was keen eyed to see them and too ... he.rted to .efend them.[38]

Throughout his life he maintained his integrity and independence. He did not belong to parties or cliques, and at all times he followed the dictates of his conscience.

Arthur's concern for the marginalized in society was a prominent and sustained feature of his life. It provides a clue to his motivation and to the stand he took on a number of issues. It prompted him to look for the liberation of American slaves, the rehabilitation of Australian aborigines, and the just treatment of black people in Jamaica who had responded to oppression with force. It deepened his commitment to education, for women in India and the deprived in British cities. It accounted too for his opposition to some of the proposals for public education in England, which seemed to favour those already enjoying power and privilege. Concern for the rights of working people in Britain led him to resist those advocating changes to the Victorian Sabbath, since the whole of an employee's week could then potentially come under the control of an employer. Arthur's opposition to juvenile prostitution in London reflected his strong sense of outrage that the strong and rich were exploiting the weak and poor. The plight of outcastes and child widows in India distressed him greatly. Allegations that mainline missionaries enjoyed a luxurious life-style in the sub-continent, remote from the vast majority of the people, touched a raw nerve. The tendency in Britain for the privileged to receive favourable handling under the law, while the vulnerable were treated harshly, offended him. Had Arthur been convinced that ordinary Catholics in Ireland were indeed the victims of injustice and oppression, and that they would benefit from proposed political and religious changes, his attitude towards the proposals might well have been different. He was not so convinced, however. Instead he believed that reality was being distorted, and that the changes would further strengthen the hand of unscrupulous politicians and priests who already wielded too much power.

Whatever uncertainties remain over aspects of Arthur's life, his motivation was consistent and clear. From his conversion in the west of Ireland till his death in Cannes, France, his one goal was to be involved in Christ's mission. This passion – to proclaim the gospel, to win souls and to promote justice – received a severe and early setback when he had to return so soon from India to Britain. As he confided to a member of his family:

> The people of my mission had become inexpressibly dear to me: I saw their woeful need of the gospel, and longed to spend my life in making it known to them. Gladly would I have resigned every hope of seeing in this life a single relation, had the Lord only counted me worthy to preach among the Gentiles the unsearchable riches of Christ. His will was otherwise.[39]

It is a tribute to Arthur's faith and spirit that despite such disappointments and difficulties he was able to accept and do God's will in the changed circumstances in which he found himself, with no trace of self-pity or bitterness. Even in the debates which raged over education and the Home Rule Bill, his guiding principle remained the furtherance of Christ's kingdom. 'He was first and last a missionary,' concluded Stephenson aptly.[40]

His Message

Methodists who, alone and with others, respond to the challenge to present Christ to a world in need, do well to become more aware of the richness of their catholic and evangelical beginnings. Methodism, as presented by Arthur, is essentially a spiritual movement committed to mission. He affirmed the primacy, urgency and comprehensive nature of mission, in which institutional as well as personal evil is taken seriously, and individual and social renewal are both encompassed. The Holy Spirit, Arthur urged, is the source of power both for personal holiness and for social transformation. Every aspect of life falls within the range of mission, including personal values and morality, the family, education, race, the economy, and national and international affairs. Vested interests must be confronted, with Christians, where necessary, taking their stand with the poor and oppressed. God, implied Arthur, is the creator of all, Christ is the redeemer of all, and the Holy Spirit is the renewer of all. Narrow national self-interest had therefore to be resisted, and a world-view promoted which affirms the essential oneness of humanity. Arthur was a member of the Royal Asiatic Society, and a fellow of the Ethnological Society,[41] positions wholly consistent for one holding such an outlook. The priorities he saw for the church in this connection included the rejection of rigid uniformity, a consensus among Christians whenever possible, and mobilizing the whole church and every believer for mission. 'The Gospel', Arthur claimed, 'is come to renew the face of the earth'.[42] It should therefore be proclaimed in all its fullness to all peoples, individuals being offered new life in Christ, and 'the general renewal of society' being constantly promoted.[43] Sectarian attitudes, coercive methods and material incentives had no place in Christian evangelism, he insisted. Intellectuals who pose a threat to Christian faith and practice should be engaged in debate, not as a mental exercise but as an aspect of mission. Yet theologians must take care not to assume that every 'new science' may 'evolve something contradictory to the Bible'.[44]

Arthur's practical interest and commitment are striking. His preaching and writing always aimed at changing people's attitudes and lives. A sermon on Hezekiah, for example, emphasized the practical nature of religious zeal. 'A man must not be judged by his power of expression in religious matters, but by his actions',[45] he declared. Hezekiah's actions influenced the life of a nation. Similarily Arthur's exposition of key Christian concepts such as the new birth, being filled with the Holy Spirit, and Christian holiness, highlighted their practical expression. 'To constitute a Christian', he wrote, 'three things are necessary – faith, experience and practice'.[46] 'It is impossible that true godliness shall spread among any people', he claimed, 'without stimulating their intellectual and social energies.'[47] The moment a man is born again, a double love is kindled in him, affirmed Arthur, love to God and love to people, none of whom are 'so deeply scarred with sin as to be beyond hope'.[48] Education aimed 'merely at the acquisition of knowledge and ignoring the power of applying it', was one-sided, he argued.[49]

Much of this remains deeply challenging today. Developments have taken place in some areas since Arthur's time. Although, for example, he favoured partnership – between nations, and within and between churches – the range and scale of partnership is now much greater than he envisaged, due to advances in thought, easier communication, greater openness and a recognition of need. The importance of contacts with people of other cultures and faiths was also recognized by Arthur, but only in a way that did not call into question or appear to compromise Christian values and Christ's uniqueness. This is a controversial area today, in which Christians are divided. Henry Haigh, who worked in Mysore for twenty-seven years from 1874, claimed in his introduction to the 1902 edition of Arthur's *A Mission to the Mysore* that Arthur's approach to people of other faiths, shared by his contemporaries, was chiefly characterized by 'uncompromising criticism, and earnest, if pitying, denunciation'.[50] Too little account was taken, Haigh submitted, of Paul's preaching at Athens (Acts 15), and of the fact that God never leaves himself anywhere without witnesses:

> In Hinduism and such like systems there is of a surety some vital truth, however hidden and entangled, the recognition of which is just and necessary, and likely to afford the best approach to the heathen man's intelligence and heart.[51]

It is a matter of judgment as to whether this is fair to Arthur or indicates an advance in his thinking. Haigh did less than justice to Arthur, however, when he expressed, as something new, a need for thoughtful Hindus to find 'a Christ' within their own systems of belief. This is no improvement on Arthur's own reference to Hindus possessing 'light from God in Christ', and on his wider reference to 'the Cross' being 'strong in the universal conscience'.[52]

It says much for Arthur that he maintained his spiritual emphasis and missionary zeal despite persistent ill health and becoming part of the Wesleyan establishment. By his person and teaching he presents a challenge to all in danger of becoming trapped in any of the institutional churches. He also provides encouragement for those who pray and strive not only for the renewal of the church but of the whole creation.

Notes

When books are listed in the Bibliography, authors are here referred to only by surname, and book titles are shortened. The Bibliography gives fuller details, including the year of publication.

The following abbreviations are used:

IWHSA Irish Wesley Historical Society Archives at Aldersgate House, Belfast

MCA Methodist Church Archives at the John Rylands Library, Manchester

In MCA entries, the details within brackets correspond to the method of classifying materials in the collection.

MMSA Methodist Missionary Society Archives at the School of Oriental and African Studies, London

In MMSA entries, the figure in brackets refers to the box number in the collection. A summary of contents for each box, as given in the handlist to the collection, is provided in the Bibliography.

UMCA The United Methodist Church Archives at Drew University, Madison, New Jersey

WMMS Wesleyan Methodist Missionary Society

Preface

1. Arthur, *The Successful Merchant*, p. ix.

1. William Arthur, 1819–1901

1. Davey, *The March of Methodism*, p. 72.
2. Turner, *Conflict and Reconciliation*, p. 107.
3. Rigg in Telford, *The Life of J. Harrison Rigg*, p. 322.
4. This is not, however, the Kells associated with the Book of Kells. Although also in Ireland, it is in Co. Meath.
5. Stephenson, *William Arthur*, p. 19.
6. Ibid., p. 18.

7. Telford, 'Death of the Rev. William Arthur', *Methodist Recorder*, 14 March 1901, p. 11.
8. Stephenson, op.cit., p. 19.
9. MCA (PLP 2.64.17.), Memorandum.
10. See, for example, Stephenson, op.cit., p. 19.
11. *Christian Advocate*, 5 October 1888, p. 481.
12. See pp. 142–44.
13. Stephenson, op.cit., p. 20.
14. Slater's *Sreet Directory*, 1846. In A. Nicholson, *Ireland's Welcome to the Stranger*, New York 1847, there is a reference to 'the kind Christian widow, Arthur, who kept the Post Office' in Newport.
15. James Arthur's name appears in the minutes of meetings of the Select Vestry for Newport Parish Church (Church of Ireland, Episcopal). For example, he paid pew rent in 1841. The last time he is mentioned is when he signed the minutes on 8 April 1844. I am grateful to the Westport Historical Society for the information in this and the previous note.
16. Woodham-Smith, *The Great Hunger*, p. 112.
17. MMSA (16), Arthur to Beecham, 25 October 1855.
18. *Christian Advocate*, 12 July 1888, p. 340.
19. *Methodist Recorder*, 7 June 1867, p. 188.
20. Arthur, *A Mission to the Mysore*, pp. 4f.
21. Ibid., pp. 47f.
22. Ibid., pp. 50f.
23. Acts 17.16; Arthur, *A Mission to the Mysore*, p. 36.
24. Arthur, *A Mission to the Mysore*, p. 63.
25. Ibid., p. 142.
26. Ibid., p. 136.
27. Ibid., p. 137.
28. Ibid., p. 139.
29. Ibid., p. 131.
30. See Hodson's letter of 15 November 1836 in WMMS *Missionary Notices*, ix, August 1837, p. 514.
31. Arthur, *A Mission to the Mysore*, p. 151.
32. Ibid., pp. 154f.
33. Ibid., p. 199.
34. Ibid., pp. 184f.
35. Ibid., p. 217; I Tim. 2.5.
36. Ibid., p. 449.
37. Ibid., pp. 449f.
38. Ibid., p. 261.
39. WMMS *Missionary Notices*, x, May 1842, pp. 104f.
40. MCA (PLP. 2.57.2.), Arthur to Hartley, 28 August 1844.
41. MCA (PLP. 2.57.14), Arthur to Rigg, 5 March 1847.

42. Ibid.
43. MCA (PLP. 2.57.19.), Arthur to Rigg, October 1847.
44. Arthur, 'The French Revolution of 1848', p. 259.
45. WMMS *Missionary Notices*, June and July 1848, pp. 106f.
46. MCA (PLP. 2.57.21.), Arthur to Rigg, May 1848.
47. *Methodist Recorder*, 14 March 1901, p. 11.
48. MCA (PLP. 2.57.22.), Arthur to Rigg, 20 July 1848.
49. *Methodist Recorder*, 14 March 1901, p. 11.
50. Arthur, *Stop the Supplies*; see also *Methodist Recorder*, 14 March 1901, p. 11.
51. Certified copy of Entry of Marriage, given at the General Register Office, London, on 13 June 1990.
52. These were among several articles said by Rigg to have been by Arthur. See his 'Appreciation' in the *Methodist Recorder*, 14 March 1901, p. 13. Internal evidence confirms Arthur as the author in some instances.
53. This point arose in correspondence between the author and Drs D.W. Bebbington and R.J. Carwardine. See Strickland (ed.), *Addresses Delivered in New York*, and Smith, *Revivalism and Social Reform*.
54. MCA (PLP. 2.58.18.), Arthur to ? (no name), 25 April 1857.
55. MCA (PLP. 2.58.19.), Arthur to ? (no name), 25 May 1857.
56. MCA (PLP. 2.58.20.), Arthur to Rigg, 25 June 1857.
57. MMSA (549), General Committee Minutes, 6 July 1860; also 20 March 1861. See too MCA (PLP. 38.68.1.), Farmer to Arthur, 7 July 1860.
58. Arthur 'The Kingdom of Italy', *London Quarterly Review*, xxiv, April and July 1865, pp. 446–492.
59. Introduction by Arthur in Milburn, *Ten Years of Preacher-Life*, p. xiv.
60. Arthur, *English Opinion on the American Rebellion*, p. 6.
61. Dickinson College, Carlisle, Pennsylvania, traces its beginnings to 1773, although its charter was granted in 1783. The college was under Presbyterian leadership until 1833, when the trustees voted to transfer it to the Baltimore Conference of the Methodist Episcopal Church. Arthur received his honorary degree, 'A.M.', from the college in 1850. His letter of acceptance is dated 16 August 1850, and is held by the college. Dickinson continues as a privately supported undergraduate liberal arts college, with about two thousand students. See also n. 37 in ch. 10.
62. *London Quarterly Review*, xxvi, April and July 1866, p. 311.
63. Arthur, *The Outbreak in Jamaica*, p. 6.
64. Ibid., p. 15.
65. *Methodist Recorder*, 26 July 1867.
66. *Methodist Recorder*, 14 March 1901, p. 14.

67. *Belfast News-Letter*, 20 August 1868; *Irish Evangelist*, September 1868, pp. 103f.
68. MCA (PLP. 2.59.18.), Arthur to Rigg, 28 August 1868.
69. MCA (PLP. 2.59.19.), Arthur to Rigg, 9 October 1868.
70. MCA (PLP. 2.59.20.), Arthur to Rigg, 10 December 1868.
71. MCA (PLP. 2.60.5.), Arthur to Rigg, 16 June 1871.
72. MCA (PLP. 2.59.19.), Arthur to Rigg, 9 October 1868.
73. MCA (PLP. 2.59.20.), Arthur to Rigg, 10 December 1868.
74. MCA (PLP. 2.59.21.), Arthur to Hoole, 5 January 1869.
75. MCA (PLP. 2.60.2.), Arthur to Hoole, 22 April 1870.
76. *Methodist Recorder*, 14 March 1901, p. 14; MCA (PLP. 2.60.3.), Arthur to Rigg, 7 January 1871.
77. MCA (PLP. 2.60.5.), Arthur to Rigg, 16 June 1871.
78. MCA (PLP. 2.60.4.), Arthur to Rigg, 10 March 1871.
79. See ch. 6.
80. MCA (PLP. 2.59.20.), Arthur to Rigg, 10 December 1868.
81. MCA (PLP. 2.60.4.), Arthur to Rigg, 10 March 1871.
82. MCA (PLP. 2.60.5.), Arthur to Rigg, 16 June 1871.
83. *Christian Advocate*, 4 January 1957, p. 4.
84. IWHSA, article by A. McCrea in *Edgehill Year Book*, p. 32 (10).
85. Arthur, *The Life of Gideon Ouseley*, p. vii.
86. *Proceedings of the Oecumenical Methodist Conference*, pp. 108, 152f., 361, 469, 495f., 578f.
87. *Proceedings of the Second Ecumenical Methodist Conference*, p. 16.
88. Arthur, *The Tongue of Fire*, p. 280.
89. *Christian Advocate*, 10 August 1888, p. 387.
90. MCA (PLP. 2.64.1.), Mary Arthur to Rigg, 5 November 1900.
91. Stephenson, op.cit., p. 126.
92. UMCA, Arthur to Crooks, 3 November 1883, in which he described how, from Cannes, he could 'look out on the Isle where Vincent of Lerins flourished, where St Patrick studied'.

2. Wesleyan Methodist

1. Davies, George, Rupp (eds), *A History of the Methodist Church* vol. 3, p. 122.
2. Arthur, *The Extent and the Moral Statistics*, p. 50.
3. Arthur, *Personal Responsibility*, p. 7.
4. Arthur, 'The Methodists and the Established Church', *London Quarterly Review*, vi, April and July 1856, p. 509.
5. Ibid., p. 512.
6. Ibid., pp. 521f.
7. Ibid., pp. 529f.
8. Ibid., pp. 530f.

9. Ibid., p. 527.
10. Arthur, *Ought Not the Two Methodist Bodies*, pp. 6f.
11. *Christian Advocate*, 4 July 1884, p. 313.
12. Arthur, 'The Methodists and the Established Church', p. 543.
13. The title of a paper read by Arthur at a Missionary Convention on 16 October 1888.
14. Arthur's article 'Christian Fellowship', *Christian Advocate*, 24 May 1888, p. 242.
15. Wesley's definition of sin in a letter to Mrs Pendarves, quoted in Rack, *Reasonable Enthusiast*, p. 399.
16. For a discussion of this point, see Rack, *Reasonable Enthusiast*, p. 400.
17. Turner, *Conflict and Reconciliation*, p. 52.
18. *Methodist Recorder*, 31 July 1866. See also *Methodist Recorder*, 6 August 1867, for a similar emphasis.
19. Bebbington, *Evangelicals in Modern Britain*, p. 153. Bebbington has since modified his position, following correspondence with the author. See his 'Holiness in Nineteenth-Century British Methodism', awaiting publication.
20. See p. 149.
21. *Irish Evangelist*, 1 December 1875, p. 143.
22. Ibid., p. 144.
23. *Christian Advocate*, 24 May 1888, p. 242.
24. *Proceedings of the Oecumenical Methodist Conference*, p. 153.
25. Arthur, *The Tongue of Fire*, pp. 131f.
26. Ibid., p. 145.
27. See discussion in an article by Rack in Davies, George, Rupp (eds), *A History of the Methodist Church* vol. 3, pp. 158–162.
28. *Christian Advocate*, 24 May 1888, p. 242.
29. Ibid.
30. Ibid.
31. *Methodist Recorder*, 28 September 1866.
32. Davies, George, Rupp (eds), *A History of the Methodist Church* vol. 4, pp. 571ff.; vol. 3, pp. 158ff.
33. *Christian Advocate*, 4 July 1884, p. 312.
34. Ibid. See too Arthur, *The Tongue of Fire*, p. 86.
35. Arthur, 'The Methodists and the Established Church', p. 528.
36. See Arthur, *The Tongue of Fire*, pp. 85ff., and 224.
37. Arthur, 'The Methodists and the Established Church', p. 520.
38. Davies, George, Rupp (eds), *A History of the Methodist Church*, vol. 4, p. 547.
39. Arthur's 'Prefatory Statement' in *Proceedings of the Oecumenical Methodist Conference*, pp. vff.
40. Ibid., pp. 69ff.

41. Arthur's 'Introduction' in *Proceedings of the Second Ecumenical Methodist Conference*, p. ix.
42. Arthur, *Ought not the Two Methodist Bodies*, pp. 3ff.
43. Ibid., pp. 6ff.
44. Ibid., p. 10. See also *Irish Evangelist*, 1 October 1877, p. 254.
45. Arthur, *Ought not the Two Methodist Bodies*, p. 20.
46. *Irish Evangelist*, 1 January 1873, p. 2.

3. Evangelical and Revivalist

1. Bebbington, *Evangelicalism in Modern Britain*, p. 3.
2. Arthur, *The Divinity of our Lord*, p. 3.
3. Ibid., p. 28.
4. Arthur, *All are Living*, p. 11.
5. Hogg (pub.), *The Wider Hope*, p. 55.
6. Ibid., p. 63. See too Arthur, *The Divinity of our Lord*, pp. 40ff.
7. MCA (PLP. 2.57.14.), Arthur to Rigg, 5 March 1847; MCA (PLP. 2.57.17.), Arthur to Rigg, 10 May 1847.
8. Arthur, *Is the Bible to Lie under a Ban*, p. 4.
9. Ibid., p. 7.
10. *Methodist Recorder*, 6 August 1867, p. 275.
11. Arthur, *The Householder's Parliament*, p. 14.
12. Arthur, *The Modern Jove*, pp. 68ff.
13. Arthur, 'The Crystal Palace', *London Quarterly Review*, iii, October 1854 and January 1855, p. 273.
14. Ibid., pp. 273f. See too Arthur, *God without Religion*, p. 34; Arthur, *The People's Day*, pp. 19, 70f.
15. Arthur, 'The Crystal Palace', p. 278.
16. Arthur, *The People's Day*, p. 69.
17. Arthur, 'The Crystal Palace', pp. 271ff.
18. Ibid., p. 271.
19. Ibid., p. 272.
20. Bebbington, *The Nonconformist Conscience*, p. 44.
21. *The Times*, 11 August 1885, p. 9.
22. Arthur, 'Hush or Speak Out?', *Christian Advocate*, 28 August 1885, p. 425.
23. Ibid., p. 426.
24. Arthur, *God without Religion*, p. 276.
25. *Methodist Recorder*, 6 August 1867, p. 276.
26. Arthur, *The Successful Merchant*, p. 259.
27. Ibid., p. 266.
28. Arthur, *The Duty of Giving away*, pp. 25f.
29. Ibid., pp. 7ff.; 31.
30. Arthur, 'The French Revolution of 1848', p. 279.

31. Carwardine, *Trans-atlantic Revivalism*, pp. 111ff.
32. Ibid., p. 133.
33. Arthur, *The Tongue of Fire*, p. 289.
34. Ibid., p. 304.
35. Ibid., p. 320.
36. Ibid., p. 332.
37. Arthur, *May we Hope for a Great Revival?*, p. 4.
38. Arthur, *The Conversion of All England*, p. 5.
39. Ibid., p. 7.
40. Ibid.
41. Arthur, *Did Christ die for All?*, pp. 11ff. See also Arthur, *The Conversion of All England*, pp. 5f.; *Free, Full, and Present Salvation*, pp. 9f.
42. Arthur, *Only Believe*, p. 11.
43. Arthur, *The Revival in Ballymena*, p. 4; *Beginnings of a Great Revival*, p. 9.
44. Arthur, *May we Hope for a Great Revival?*, p. 8.
45. Ibid., pp. 14f.
46. Ibid., pp. 5, 14.
47. Arthur, *The Revival in Ballymena*, p. 10.
48. MMSA (17), Arthur to Hoole, 30 June 1859.
49. Arthur, *The Revival in Ulster*, p. 4; and Psalm 32.3.
50. *Wesleyan Times*, 26 March 1860, p. 197.
51. Nelson, *The Year of Delusion*, p. 189.
52. Ibid., p. 193.
53. Macaulay, *Patrick Dorrian, Bishop*, pp. 80, 84, 163f.
54. *Methodist Recorder*, 31 July 1866.
55. *Methodist Recorder*, 2 May 1867.
56. *Methodist Recorder*, 7 June 1867, p. 186.
57. *Methodist Recorder*, 6 August 1867, p. 275.
58. *Methodist Recorder*, 7 June 1867, p. 186.
59. Arthur, *The Tongue of Fire*, p. 67.
60. *Proceedings of the Second Ecumenical Methodist Conference*, p. 20.
61. Arthur, *The Tongue of Fire*, pp. 86f.
62. *Report of the Proceedings of the (inaugural) Conference*, p. 363.
63. Arthur, *Personal Responsibility*, pp. 10f.
64. Ibid., p. 11.
65. Arthur, *The Extent and the Moral Statistics*, p. 56.
66. Ibid., p. 29.

4. Communicator

1. Telford, 'Death of the Rev. William Arthur', *Methodist Recorder*, 14 March 1901, p. 11.

2. *Christian Advocate* (New York), 5 November 1891, p. 2. See too Arthur, *The Duty of Giving away*, p. 3.
3. MCA (PLP. 2.57.20.), Arthur, n.d.
4. Ibid.
5. *Methodist Recorder*, 14 March 1901, p. 11.
6. Telford, *The Life of J. Harrison Rigg*, p. 33.
7. *Methodist Recorder*, 14 March 1901, p. 11.
8. *London Quarterly Review*, xii, April and July 1859, p. 531.
9. Ibid., pp. 531, 538.
10. Ibid., pp. 529f.
11. Ibid., p. 536.
12. Arthur, *The Tongue of Fire*, p. 309.
13. Ibid., p. 312.
14. *London Quarterly Review*, vi, April and July 1856, p. 399.
15. Kendall, *Pulpit Liberty*, p. 6.
16. Ibid., pp. 6f.
17. Ibid., p. 10.
18. Arthur, *The Tongue of Fire*, p. 244.
19. Ibid., p. 246. The Leyden jar was a device for storing static electricity. It is of importance as a prototype of the capacitor.
20. Ibid., p. 299.
21. Ibid., p. 240.
22. Ibid., p. 255.
23. *Christian Advocate*, 25 December 1891, p. 616. See also *Methodist Recorder*, 6 August 1867, p. 275; Gal. 4.19.
24. Arthur, 'Jabez Bunting', *London Quarterly Review*, xii, April and July 1859, p. 538.
25. Arthur, *A Mission to the Mysore*, pp. 233f.
26. L.L. Morris's article, 'Atonement', in the *New Dictionary of Theology*, p. 55.
27. Arthur, 'God's Anger with the Wicked', pp. 503f.
28. Ibid., pp. 507f.
29. Rigg, 'Appreciation', *Methodist Recorder*, 14 March 1901, p. 12.
30. Ibid.
31. Arthur, *The Tongue of Fire*, p. 234.
32. Ibid., p. 235.
33. Ibid., pp. 243, 263.
34. Ibid., pp. 20f.
35. *Wesleyan Times*, 12 January 1852, p. 28.
36. *Wesleyan Times*, 20 October 1856, p. 658.
37. Arthur, *The Life of Gideon Ouseley*, p. ix.
38. Arthur, *The Tongue of Fire*, pp. 300f.
39. Bebbington, 'Holiness in Nineteenth-Century British Methodism', unpublished, p. 5.

40. Stephenson, *William Arthur*, p. 109.

5. Missionary

1. Arthur, *A Mission to the Mysore*, London 1847.
2. Arthur, *The Twentieth Century in the View of Mission Work and Workers*, London 1899.
3. Arthur admitted of Van Diemen's Land (Tasmania) that it was 'stained with . . . horrible wrong'. This, he acknowledged, was 'one of the many ensanguined records in colonial history'. See Arthur, *The Extent and the Moral Statistics*, p. 25.
4. WMMS *Missionary Notices*, June and July 1848, p. 103. Arthur believed that Britain's possessions in India 'were perfectly unaccountable except upon the supposition that it was the result of the hand of God being with us'. See Arthur, '*British India*', p. 18; *The Conversion of All England*, p. 2.
5. Arthur, *Shall the Loyal be Deserted*, p. 37.
6. Taggart, *The Irish in World Methodism*, especially pp. 87–103.
7. Arthur, 'Christian Hatred', *Methodist Recorder*, 2 June 1865, p. 178.
8. Arthur, *A Mission to the Mysore*, pp. 283f.
9. Arthur, *The Outbreak in Jamaica*, p. 5.
10. Arthur, *The Extent and the Moral Statistics*, pp. 47f.
11. Arthur, *A Mission to the Mysore*, p. 64.
12. Ibid., p. 285.
13. Ibid., p. 362.
14. Ibid., pp. 160f. See too pp. 348ff.
15. Ibid., p. 353.
16. Ibid., p. 305.
17. Arthur, *Women's Work in India*, p. 39.
18. Arthur, '*British India*', p. 25.
19. Taggart, op.cit., pp. 92ff.
20. Arthur, *A Mission to the Mysore*, pp. 379, 400, 407, 413.
21. Ibid., p. 391.
22. Ibid., pp. 404f.
23. Arthur, *God without Religion*, p. 81.
24. Arthur, 'Mohammedanism', p. 129.
25. Arthur, *A Mission to the Mysore*, p. 447.
26. See p. 59.
27. Arthur, *A Mission to the Mysore*, p. 231; *The Conversion of All England*, p. 7.
28. Arthur, *A Mission to the Mysore*, p. 201.
29. Ibid., pp. 260f.
30. Arthur, *The Tongue of Fire*, pp. 130f.
31. Arthur, *A Mission to the Mysore*, pp. 261f.

32. Ibid., pp. 262f.
33. See pp. 48f., 80, 84–86 above; and 140, 153f. below.
34. Smith, 'A Historical Study of the Protestant Use of the Bible', p. 54.
35. *Proceedings of the Oecumenical Methodist Conference*, p. 495.
36. Arthur, *Italy in Transition*, p. 266. See too *London Quarterly Review*, xxvi, April and July 1866, pp. 278f. for references to 'Divine strategy' and 'Divine Method' in freeing slaves in America.
37. *The Missionary Controversy: Discussion, Evidence and Report* is the official record relating to the controversy.
38. Ibid., pp. 4ff.
39. Ibid., p. 6.
40. Ibid., pp. 10ff.
41. Ibid., pp. 376ff.
42. Ibid., p. 388.
43. WMMS *Missionary Notices*, February 1896, p. 18.
44. *Evangelical Alliance, Annual Reports, 1848–1869* (bound volume). At the eighth annual conference in 1854, Arthur welcomed the sending of missionaries to countries where the gospel 'had been perverted and almost lost . . . so that the flame of Christianity might be re-lit in the ancient Churches'.
45. E.E. Jenkins, 'William Arthur', in *London Quarterly Review*, July 1901, p. 61.

6. Controversialist: Education

1. MCA (PLP. 2.59.20.), Arthur to Rigg, 10 December 1868.
2. *Belfast News-Letter*, 20 August 1868; *Irish Evangelist*, September 1868, pp. 102–104.
3. *Irish Evangelist*, September 1868, p. 103.
4. Ibid., p. 104.
5. Ibid.
6. Ibid., pp. 103f.
7. Ibid., p. 104.
8. Telford, *The Life of J. Harrison Rigg*, p. 170.
9. MCA (PLP. 2.59.20.), Arthur to Rigg, 10 December 1868.
10. MCA (PLP. 2.59.23.), Arthur to Rigg, 23 October 1869.
11. Telford, *The Life of J. Harrison Rigg*, p. 174.
12. Ibid., p. 176.
13. MCA (PLP. 2.60.4.), Arthur to Rigg, 10 March 1871.
14. MCA (PLP. 2.60.7.), Arthur to Rigg, 25 October 1871.
15. Telford, *The Life of J. Harrison Rigg*, p. 181. See also *Irish Evangelist*, September 1872, p. 106.
16. Telford, *The Life of J. Harrison Rigg*, p. 182.
17. *Irish Evangelist*, 1 January 1873, pp. 1ff.

18. Bebbington, *The Nonconformist Conscience*, p. 129.
19. *Irish Evangelist*, 1 January 1873, p. 2.
20. Telford, *The Life of J. Harrison Rigg*, p. 182.
21. Ibid.
22. Davies, George, Rupp (eds), *A History of the Methodist Church* vol. 3, p. 149.
23. Telford, *The Life of J. Harrison Rigg*, p. 183.
24. Ibid., pp. 322f.
25. *Irish Evangelist*, February 1869, p. 13.
26. Ibid.
27. *Irish Evangelist*, April 1869, p. 40. See also Macaulay, *Patrick Dorrian, Bishop*, pp. 260ff.
28. *Irish Evangelist*, April 1869, p. 40.
29. Ibid., p. 41.
30. Macaulay, op.cit., pp. 260ff.
31. *Irish Evangelist*, April 1870, p. 45.
32. Macaulay, op.cit., pp. 264f.
33. G.F.A. Best, quoted in Hempton, *Methodism and Politics in British Society*, p. 149.
34. Hempton, ibid.
35. G.F.A. Best, quoted in Hempton, ibid.
36. Bebbington, *The Nonconformist Conscience*, p. 131.

7. Controversialist: Politics

1. Bebbington, *The Nonconformist Conscience*, p. 11.
2. For discussions on the 'no politics' tradition, see *Christian Advocate*, 12 May 1887, pp. 223f.; and 28 June 1892, pp. 331f. See also Arthur, *An Explanation*, pp. 5ff.
3. Arthur, *The Householder's Parliament*, p. 11.
4. Bebbington, *The Nonconformist Conscience*, p. 101. Parnell's adulterous relationship with Mrs O'Shea offended many people. Nonconformist pressure on Gladstone influenced him to make a public statement, that he thought Parnell should cease to lead the Irish party in parliament.
5. *Christian Advocate*, 4 June 1886, p. 271.
6. Hempton, ' "For God and Ulster" ', p. 245.
7. *Christian Advocate*, 24 December 1885, p. 639. See also 8 January 1886, p. 19; 29 January 1886, p. 55.
8. Ibid., 8 January 1886, p. 19.
9. Ibid., 15 January 1886, p. 31.
10. Ibid., 22 January 1886, pp. 42f.
11. Ibid., 29 June 1886, p. 322.
12. Ibid., 2 July 1886, p. 331.

13. Ibid., 30 April 1886, pp. 211f.
14. Arthur, *Shall the Loyal be Deserted*, pp. 10ff., 34f.
15. Ibid., p. 34.
16. Ibid., p. 17.
17. Ibid., pp. 28ff. See also *Christian Advocate*, 8 January 1886, p. 19; Arthur, *Moral Points in the Home Rule Controversy*, pp. 7f.
18. Arthur, *Shall the Loyal be Deserted*, p. 29.
19. MCA (PLP. 2.61.7.), Arthur to Hargraves, 9 July 1886.
20. See, for example, Arthur, *Shall the Loyal be Deserted*, pp. 9, 17, 18, and 19.
21. Ibid., pp. 14f.
22. Ibid., pp. 27f.
23. Ibid., p. 36.
24. *The Times*, 30 June 1886.
25. Arthur, *An Explanation*, pp. 6f. See also *Christian Advocate*, 13 August 1886, p. 400.
26. Arthur, *An Explanation*, p. 5.
27. Bebbington, *The Nonconformist Conscience*, p. 92.
28. Edwards, *Methodism and England*, p. 167; *Christian Advocate*, 28 June 1892, p. 332.
29. *Christian Advocate*, 22 January 1886, p. 43.
30. Ibid., 5 February 1886, p. 67.
31. Ibid., 19 April 1888, p. 188.
32. Bebbington, *The Nonconformist Conscience*, pp. 84, 99. For the dominant Irish Wesleyan attitude towards Hughes, see, for example, *Christian Advocate*, 14 August 1891, p. 392.
33. Arthur, *Moral Points*, p. 3; *Christian Advocate*, 30 January 1891, pp. 50f.
34. Arthur, *Moral Points*, p. 13.
35. MCA (PLP. 2.61.7.), Arthur to Hargraves, 9 July 1886.
36. *Christian Advocate*, 24 June 1892, p. 329. See too Arthur, *The Householder's Parliament*, pp. 11f.
37. *Christian Advocate*, 2 September 1892, pp. 446f.; 9 September 1892, pp. 460f.; 21 October 1892, pp. 530f.
38. Rogers, *The Ulster Problem*, pp. 7ff.
39. Ibid., pp. 5, 21, 31.
40. Ibid., p. 29.
41. Ibid., p. 5.
42. Ibid., p. 8.
43. Ibid., p. 9.
44. Ibid., pp. 12f.
45. Ibid., p. 22.
46. Ibid., pp. 19f.
47. Ibid., p. 24.

48. The 'Prefatory Note' at the beginning of Arthur's pamphlet, *Shall the Loyal be Deserted and the Disloyal set over Them?*, presents Parnell as a person mistrusted and feared not only by loyalists and Protestants, but by fair-minded people generally. For a more sympathetic study of Parnell, see Lyons, *Charles Stuart Parnell*.

8. Apologist

1. A.S. Wood's article 'Methodism' in the *New Dictionary of Theology*, p. 427.
2. UMCA, Arthur to Crooks, 31 August 1883.
3. Ibid. See also Arthur, *On the Difference between Physical and Moral Law*, p. 6.
4. Ibid., pp. 9f.
5. Ibid., p. 221.
6. Arthur, *Religion without God*, p. 43.
7. Ibid., pp. 6ff.
8. Arthur, *God without Religion*, pp. 215f., 388ff., 415f., 421; *Religion without God*, pp. 521ff.
9. Arthur, *God without Religion*, p. 200.
10. Arthur, *On Time and Space*, p. 214.
11. Arthur, *God without Religion*, p. v.
12. Arthur, *Religion without God*, pp. 39; 132.
13. Ibid., pp. 50ff.

9. William Arthur and Roman Catholicism

1. Hempton, *Methodism and Politics*, pp. 28f., 35ff.
2. Hempton, ' "For God and Ulster" ', p. 249.
3. Bebbington, *The Nonconformist Conscience*, pp. 90f.
4. Connolly, *Religion and Society*, pp. 36f. See also *Christian Advocate*, 15 July 1892, p. 368; 2 September 1892, p. 447.
5. *Christian Advocate*, 30 January 1891, p. 51; 28 June 1892, p. 327. See also Arthur, *Moral Points*, p. 10.
6. Arthur, *Shall the Loyal be Deserted*, p. 38.
7. *Christian Advocate*, 21 June 1892, p. 305. It is interesting to note, however, that a relative of T.F. Shillington, Thomas Shillington, had been the unsuccessful, pro-Home Rule, Ulster Liberal candidate in the 1885 General Election, standing in the North Armagh constituency. See Walker, *Ulster Politics*, pp. 197, 213, 216, 236 and 251f.
8. Hempton, ' "For God and Ulster" ', p. 234.
9. Stephenson, *William Arthur*, p. 21.

10. Arthur, 'Ultramontanism', *London Quarterly Review*, i, September and December 1853, p. 215.
11. Arthur, *Italy in Transition*, p. 330.
12. Ibid., p. 345.
13. Ibid., p. 168.
14. Ibid., pp. 161ff.
15. Ibid., p. 380.
16. E. di Campello, *Count Campello*, pp. xv, xviii.
17. Arthur, *Italy in Transition*, pp. 263f.
18. *London Quarterly Review*, xxiv, April and July 1865, pp. 491f.
19. Ibid., l, April and July 1878, p. 114.
20. Ibid., pp. 114ff.
21. Ibid., pp. 125, 140, 143.
22. Ibid., pp. 130f.
23. Ibid., pp. 142f.
24. Arthur, *The Pope, the Kings, and the People*, p. xxi.
25. Ibid., pp. xxif.
26. Ibid., pp. 671ff.
27. *Irish Evangelist*, 1 December 1873, pp. 133f.
28. Arthur (trans.), *Authentic Report of the Discussion*, pp. 3ff.
29. Ibid., p. 9.
30. *The Times*, 21 February 1872, p. 4.
31. *The Times*, 18 March 1872.
32. Wesley's sermon, 'A Caution against Bigotry', quoted in *Irish Evangelist*, 1 August 1878, p. 376; also *Christian Advocate*, 4 March 1892, p. 115.
33. *Christian Advocate*, 23 October 1891, p. 509.
34. *Irish Evangelist*, 1 August 1879, p. 513.
35. Ibid.
36. *Christian Advocate*, 23 October 1891, p. 509.
37. Quoted in *Irish Evangelist*, 1 August 1878, p. 376.
38. Arthur, *The Extent and the Moral Statistics*, pp. 27f.
39. Rigg, 'Appreciation', *Methodist Recorder*, 14 March 1901, p. 14.
40. Connolly, *Religion and Society in Nineteenth-Century Ireland*, p. 13.
41. *Christian Advocate*, 6 November 1891, p. 533.

10. The Man and his Message

1. The article in the Supplement (January 1901 – December 1911) to the *Dictionary of National Biography* says that the Arthurs had six daughters. Stephenson says they had four. See his *William Arthur*, p. 121. I believe that five is the correct number.
2. *Methodist Recorder*, 14 March 1901, p. 12.
3. *Methodist Recorder*, 24 August 1866.

4. *Christian Advocate*, 12 July 1888, p. 340.

5. Arthur, *A Mission to the Mysore*, p. 261.

6. MMSA (16), Arthur to Beecham, 11 September 1855.

7. MMSA (16), Arthur to Beecham, 25 October 1855.

8. *Methodist Recorder*, 14 March 1901, p. 12. The Star Life Assurance Society was founded in 1843 specifically to appeal to Wesleyan Methodists.

9. Arthur, *Italy in Transition*, p. xii.

10. See pp. 30f.

11. MCA (PLP. 2.57.23.), Arthur to Rigg, 11 October 1848.

12. MMSA (16), Arthur to Hoole, 7 October 1856.

13. 'Probate of the Will of Miss Agnes Morley Arthur, Deceased', dated 30 November 1934, p. 5, extracted by Allen and Overy, 3 Finch Lane, EC3.

14. MCA (PLP. 2.60.3.), Arthur to Rigg, 7 January 1871; and *Methodist Recorder*, 14 March 1901, p. 14.

15. Telford, *The Life of J. Harrison Rigg* – see, for example, pp. 37f., 52f., 57, 72f., 86f., 161, 170, 173ff., 279f.

16. *Methodist Recorder*, 14 March 1901, p. 12.

17. Ibid.

18. Telford, *The Life of J. Harrison Rigg*, pp. 33f.

19. MCA (PLP. 2.57.8.), Arthur to Rigg, 20 December 1845.

20. Telford, *The Life of J. Harrison Rigg*, pp. 72f.

21. Ibid., p. 57.

22. Ibid., p. 170.

23. *Methodist Recorder*, 14 March 1901, p. 12.

24. Ibid.

25. MCA (PLP. 2.62.8.), Arthur to Rigg, 3 June 1897.

26. *Methodist Recorder*, 14 March 1901, p. 12.

27. *Proceedings of the Second Ecumenical Methodist Conference*, p. 261.

28. Arthur, *The Successful Merchant*, pp. 370f.

29. *Methodist Recorder*, 14 March 1901, p. 14.

30. Ibid., p. 12.

31. I have been unable to trace the source of this information.

32. MCA (PLP. 2.57.22.), Arthur to Rigg, 20 July 1848.

33. *Methodist Recorder*, 14 March 1901, p. 14.

34. Jenkins, 'William Arthur', *London Quarterly Review*, July 1901, pp. 62, 67f.

35. Ibid., p. 68.

36. *Methodist Recorder*, 14 March 1901, p. 12.

37. I am grateful to Dickinson College for this information, and for the information contained in n. 61 in ch. 1. The degree declined in 1856 was a DD.

38. *Methodist Recorder*, 14 March 1901, p. 11.

39. Arthur, *A Mission to the Mysore*, p. 450.
40. Stephenson, *William Arthur*, p. 45.
41. See flyleaf of Arthur, *What is Fiji?*
42. Arthur, *The Tongue of Fire*, p. 133.
43. Ibid., p. 132.
44. Arthur, 'The French Revolution', p. 275.
45. Arthur, *Two Sermons preached*, p. 5.
46. Arthur, *The Tongue of Fire*, p. 218.
47. Ibid., p. 329.
48. Arthur, *Two Sermons preached*, p. 8.
49. *Irish Evangelist*, September 1868, p. 103.
50. In Arthur, *A Mission to the Mysore*, pp. viif.
51. Ibid., p. viii.
52. See the discussion on pp. 85f., with the notes.

Bibliography

1. PRIMARY SOURCES

(a) Manuscripts

(b) Reports

(c) Newspapers and periodicals

2. THE WRITINGS OF WILLIAM ARTHUR

(a) Books

(b) Pamphlets

(c) Introductions and prefaces

(d) Other material

3. OTHER WORKS

(a) Books and pamphlets

(b) Articles

(c) Theses

1. PRIMARY SOURCES

(a) Manuscripts

Methodist Missionary Society Archives (MMSA) at the School of Oriental and African Studies, London

Box List:-

16 Home Correspondence 1855–1856

24 Outgoing Letters 3. 1820–1845

25 Outgoing Letters 4. 1845–1854; 1855–1867

26 Outgoing Letters 5. 1864–1877

   27 Outgoing Letters 6. (District General) 1884–1895
   29 Outgoing Letters 8. (District General Letters) 1891–1906
   38 Outgoing Letters 17. (Section – Ireland; Canada; Australia) 1881–1907
   46 Circulars 1819–1882; 1841–1845; 1877–1890; 1847–1904
   62 France Correspondence 1844–1863
   76 Ireland Correspondence 1858–1862
  354 India Synod Minutes 1824–1855
  427 Correspondence – Mysore 1835–1857
  537 Fiji Correspondence 1855–1860
  549 Minutes General 5. 1837–1865
  550 Minutes General 6. 1865–1880
  553 Minutes General 7c. 1867–1884
  554 Minutes General 8. 1884–1888
  555 Minutes General 9. 1888–1892
  556 Minutes General 10. 1892–1897
  557 Minutes General 11. 1897–1902
  661 Candidates 2b. 1845–1869
 1104 Women's Work Minutes 1. 1858–1890
 1105 Women's Work Minutes 2. 1891–1907

Methodist Church Archives (MCA) at the John Rylands University Library, Manchester
   William Arthur Papers
   James H. Rigg Papers

The Archives and History Center of the United Methodist Church (UMCA) at Drew University, Madison, New Jersey
   William Arthur Papers

Irish Wesley Historical Society Archives (IWHSA) at Aldersgate House, Belfast
   Minute Book of Hibernian Auxiliary to WMMS, 1861–1923

Library of United Theological College, Bangalore, India
   Synod Minutes (Methodist)

Mission House, Gubbi, India
   Baptismal Register, 20 July 1837–1950s

(b) Reports

Evangelical Alliance, Annual Reports
Minutes of the Methodist Conferences (Primitive Wesleyan, and Wesleyan, in Ireland)
Minutes of the Methodist Conferences (Wesleyan, Britain)
Proceedings of the Oecumenical Methodist Conference, London 1881
Proceedings of the Second Ecumenical Methodist Conference, London 1892
Report of the Proceedings of the (inaugural) Conference, 1846, Evangelical Alliance
Reports of Hibernian Auxiliary of the WMMS
The Missionary Controversy: Discussion, Evidence and Report, London 1890
WMMS *Annual Reports*

(c) Newspapers and periodicals

Christian Advocate (Ireland)
Christian Guardian (Canada)
Evangelical Christendom
Irish Evangelist
London Quarterly Review
Methodist Recorder
Methodist Times
WMMS *Missionary Notices*
WMMS *Women's Work Occasional (or Quarterly) Papers*

2. THE WRITINGS OF WILLIAM ARTHUR

(a) Books

A Mission to the Mysore, London 1847
Authentic Report of the Discussion held in Rome (trans.), London 1872
Italy in Transition, London 1860
On the Difference between Physical and Moral Law, London 1883
Religion without God and *God without Religion*, London 1885–88
   (initially in three parts)
The Life of Gideon Ouseley, London 1876
The Modern Jove, London 1873
The Pope, the Kings, and the People, London 1877
The Successful Merchant, London 1852

The Tongue of Fire, London 1856
Women's Work in India, London 1882

(b) Pamphlets

Afghanistan: in relation to Past Conquests of India, Westminster 1879
All are Living, London 1853
An Explanation, London 1886
Beginnings of a Great Revival, London 1859
Did Christ die for All?, London 1859
Free, Full and Present Salvation, London n.d.
God's Anger with the Wicked, London 1856
Has the Conference broken Covenant?, London 1852
Is the Bible to Lie under a Ban in India?, London 1859
May we Hope for a Great Revival?, London 1859
Methodism and the Established Church, London 1868
Moral Points in the Home Rule Controversy, London 1891
On Class Meeting: or Christian Fellowship . . ., London 1888
On Time and Space, Two Witnesses for a Creator, London 1887
Only Believe, London n.d.
Ought not the Two Methodist Bodies in Ireland to become One?, Dublin
  1869
Personal Responsibility in Relation to the Evangelical Alliance, London
  1850
Shall the Loyal be Deserted and the Disloyal set over Them?, London
  1886
Stop the Supplies, London 1849
*The American Question: 1 English Opinion on the American Rebellion
  . . .*, London 1861
The Best of Causes, London 1888
The Conversion of All England, London 1859
The Divinity of our Lord in Relation to His Work of Atonement, London
  1885
The Duty of Giving away a Stated Proportion of our Income, London
  1855
The Extent and the Moral Statistics of the British Empire, London 1845
The Householder's Parliament, London 1885
The Outbreak in Jamaica, London 1865
The People's Day, London 1855
The Revival in Ballymena and Coleraine, London 1859
The Revival in Ulster: Ahoghill and Ballymena, London 1859
The Twentieth Century in the View of Mission Work and Workers,
  London 1899

Two Sermons preached by . . . W. Arthur . . . and L.H. Wiseman, Southport 1861
What is Fiji?, London 1859

(c) Introductions and prefaces

Proceedings of the Oecumenical Methodist Conference, London 1881
Proceedings of the Second Ecumenical Methodist Conference, London 1892
Benrath, Carl, *Bernadino Ochino of Siena*, London 1876
Briggs, F.W., *Chequer Alley*, London 1866
Campello, E. di, *Count Campello*, London 1881
Dobbin, O.T., *Wesley the Worthy*, London 1852
Fisch, G., *Nine Months in the United States*, London 1863
Hodson, T., *Old Daniel*, London 1877
Macafee, D., *The Pillar and the Ground of the Truth*, London 1872
Milburn, W.H., *Ten Years of Preacher-Life*, London 1859
Moister, W., *The Father of our Missions*, London 1871
Toase, W., *Memorials of the Rev. William Toase*, London 1874

(d) Other material

'Abraham Lincoln', *London Quarterly Review*, xxvi, April and July 1866, pp. 269–315
'British India', YMCA, *Lectures delivered . . . 1845*, London 1864, pp. 3–30
'Christian Hatred', *Methodist Recorder*, 2 June 1865
'God's Anger with the Wicked', YMCA, Exeter Hall Sunday Evening Lectures, viii, 1856, pp. 503–510
'Heroes', YMCA, *Twelve Lectures . . .*, London 1851
Hogg, James (pub.), *The Wider Hope*, London 1890, chapter 4
'Hush or Speak Out?', *Christian Advocate*, 28 August 1885
'Jabez Bunting', *London Quarterly Review*, xii, April and July 1859, pp. 513–44
Letter, *Irish Evangelist*, April 1870
Letters to Editor, *Daily News*, published in *Irish Evangelist*, February 1869, April 1869 and August 1869
'Methodism, a Power Purifying and Elevating Society', *Proceedings of the Oecumenical Methodist Conference*, London 1881, pp. 69–78
'Mohammedanism', YMCA, *Lectures delivered . . . 1847-8*, London 1848, pp. 95–130
Opening Sermon, *Proceedings of the Second Ecumenical Methodist Conference*, London 1892, pp. 3–26

'Our Recent Gains an Earnest of Future and Greater Gains', *Canadian Methodist Magazine*, January to June 1877

'Religious Exercises of a Church Truly Apostolic', *Christian Guardian* (Canada), 6 May 1868

Sermon, *Methodist Recorder*, 21 September 1866

Sermon, *Methodist Recorder*, 6 August 1867

Sermon, *Sermons by Wesleyan Methodist Ministers*, ii, London 1851

'Spinoza', *London Quarterly Review*, xlviii, April and July 1877, pp. 124–52

'The Church in the Catecombs', YMCA, *Twelve Lectures* . . ., London 1850

'The Crystal Palace', *London Quarterly Review*, iii, October 1854 and January 1855, pp. 232–79

'The Dangers and Right Use of Commercial Prosperity', W.H.R., *Religion in its Relation to Commerce* . . ., London 1852

'The Deed of Declaration and the Centenary of Methodism in America', *Christian Advocate*, 4 July 1884

'The Field is the World', WMMS *Missionary Notices*, February 1896

'The French Revolution of 1848', YMCA, *Lectures to Young Men* . . ., London 1849, pp. 251–280

'The Kingdom of Italy', *London Quarterly Review*, xxiv, April and July 1865, pp. 446–92

'The Lord's Supper', *Christian Advocate*, 17 August 1888

'The Methodists and the Established Church', *London Quarterly Review*, vi, April and July 1856, pp. 508–45

'The Political Struggle in Germany', *Irish Evangelist*, 1 December 1873

'The Pope's Encyclical', *London Quarterly Review*, xxiv, April and July 1865, 79–105

'The State of Papal Europe', *Evangelical Christendom*, 1 December 1876

'The Vatican and the Kremlin', *London Quarterly Review*, xxvi, October 1865 and January 1866, pp. 89–135

'Ultramontanism: Its threatened Supremacy in Europe', *London Quarterly Review*, i, September and December 1853, pp. 214–32

3. OTHER WORKS

(a) Books and pamphlets

Bebbington, D.W., *Evangelicals in Modern Britain*, London 1989

Bebbington, D.W., *The Nonconformist Conscience*, London 1982

Beckett, J.C., *The Making of Modern Ireland 1603–1923*, London 1966

Brash, W. Bardsley, *The Story of our Colleges 1835–1935*, London 1935

Carson, J.T., *God's River in Spate*, Belfast 1958

Carwardine, Richard, *Trans-atlantic Revivalism – Popular Evangelicalism in Britain and America, 1790–1865*, Westport, Connecticut 1978

Caughey, James, *Revival Sermons and Addresses*, London 1891

Cole, R.L., *History of methodism in Ireland*, Belfast 1960

Connolly, Sean, *Religion and Society in Nineteenth Century Ireland*, Dundalk 1985

Crook, William, *Ireland and the Centenary of American Methodism*, London 1866

Crookshank, C.H., *History of Methodism in Ireland*, iii, London 1888

Curtis, Edmund, *A History of Ireland*, London 1936

Davey, Cyril J., *The March of Methodism*, London 1951

Davies, R.E., *Methodism*, London 1964

Davies, R.E. and E.G. Rupp (eds), *A History of the Methodist Church in Great Britain*, vol. 1, London 1965

Davies, R.E., A.R. George and E.G. Rupp (eds), *A History of the Methodist Church in Great Britain*, vol. 2, London 1978; vol. 3, London 1983; vol. 4, London 1988

Edwards, Maldwyn, *Methodism and England: A Study of Methodism in its Social and Political Aspects 1850–1932*, London 1943

Findlay, G.G. and M.G. Findlay, *Wesley's World Parish*, London 1913

Findlay, G.G. and W.W. Holdsworth, *The History of the Wesleyan Methodist Missionary Society*, 5 volumes, London 1921–24

Goodall, N., *Christian Missions and Social Ferment*, London 1964

Gregory, Benjamin, *Side-Lights on the Conflicts of Methodism 1827–52*, London 1898

Harmon, Nolan B. (ed.), *The Encyclopedia of World Methodism*, 2 volumes, Nashville 1974

Hempton, David, *Methodism and Politics in British Society*, London 1984

Hempton, David and Hill, Myrtle, *Evangelical Protestantism in Ulster Society 1740–1890*, London 1992

Henderson, J.W., *Methodist College, Belfast*, Belfast 1939

Holt, I.L. and E.T. Clark, *The World Methodist Movement*, Nashville 1956

Hoole, E., *Missions in Madras, Mysore and the South of India*, London 1844

Jeffery, F., *Irish Methodism*, Belfast 1964

Kendall, James, *Pulpit Liberty: or Notes on some remarkable passages in 'The Tongue of Fire'*, London 1857

Kent, J.H.S., *Holding the Fort: Studies in Victorian Revivalism*, London 1978

Lee, Joseph, *The Modernisation of Irish Society 1848–1918*, Dublin 1973

Lyons, F.S.L., *Ireland Since the Famine*, Glasgow 1971

Lyons, F.S.L., *Charles Stuart Parnell*, London 1977

Macaulay, Ambrose, *Patrick Dorrian, Bishop of Down and Connor 1865–1885*, Dublin 1987

Marshall, Ronald, *Methodist College Belfast*, Belfast n.d.

Moody, T.W. and Beckett, J.C., *Ulster since 1800*, London 1957

Moody, T.W., and F.X. Martin (eds), *The Course of Irish History*, Cork 1967

Neill, S., G.H. Anderson and J. Godwin (eds), *Concise Dictionary of Christian World Mission*, London 1970

Nelson, Isaac, *The Year of Delusion*, Belfast 1861

Prescott, Peter, *Methodism in Relation to Popery: a letter to the Rev. W. Arthur*, London 1880

Rack, Henry D., *Reasonable Enthusiast: John Wesley and the Rise of Methodism*, London 1989, 2nd edn 1992

Rogers, J. Guinness, *The Ulster Problem*, London 1886

Semmel, B., *The Methodist Revolution*, London 1974

Smith, T.L., *Revivalism and Social Reform: American Protestantism on the Eve of the Civil War*, New York 1965

Stephenson, T. Bowman, *William Arthur*, London 1907

Strickland, W.P. (ed.), *Addresses Delivered in New York by Rev. William Arthur, A.M.*, New York 1856

T.H. (Thomas Hughes), *A Defence and a Plea*, London 1870

Taggart, Norman W., *The Irish in World Methodism 1760–1900*, London 1986

Telford, John, *A Short History of Wesleyan Methodist Foreign Missions*, London 1905

Telford, John, *The Life of J. Harrison Rigg, D.D.*, London 1909

Townsend, W.J., H.B. Workman and G. Eayrs (eds), *A New History of Methodism*, 2 volumes, London 1909

Turner, J.M., *Conflict and Reconciliation: Studies in Methodism and Ecumenism in England 1740–1982*, London 1985

Wakefield, G.S., *Methodist Devotion*, London 1966

Walker, B.M., *Ulster Politics: the Formative Years 1868–1886*, Belfast 1989

Warren, Max, *Social History and Christian Mission*, London 1967

Warren, Max, *The Missionary Movement from Britain in Modern History*, London 1965

Woodham-Smith, Cecil, *The Great Hunger*, London 1962

(b) Articles

Valuable background material is found in the *Proceedings of the Wesley Historical Society* and in *Methodist History* (published in the U.S.A.)

Bebbington, D.W., 'Holiness in Nineteenth-Century British Methodism', unpublished, 1991

Hempton, David, 'The Methodist Crusade in Ireland 1795–1845', *Irish Historical Studies*, xxii no. 85, March 1980, pp. 33–48

Hempton, David, ' "For God and Ulster": Evangelical Protestantism and the Home Rule Crisis of 1886', *Studies in Church History*, Subsidia 7, 1990, pp. 225–54

Hempton, David, 'Gideon Ouseley: rural revivalist, 1791–1839', *Studies in Church History*, 25, 1989, pp. 203–14

Macquiban, Tim S.A., 'The British Methodist Press and Attitudes to Italy in the Period prior to 1861', unpublished, 1991

Stephens, W.P., 'The British Origins of the Italian Methodist Church', unpublished, 1991

Wood, A. Skevington, *Love Excluding Sin* (Wesley's Doctrine of Sanctification), Wesley Fellowship, n.d.

(c) Theses

Lists of academic theses have appeared in the *Proceedings of the Wesley Historical Society* at intervals since March 1963

Binns, J.R., *A History of Methodism in Ireland*, MA thesis, Queen's University, Belfast 1960

Megahey, Alan J., *The Irish Protestant Churches and Social and Political Issues 1870–1914*, Ph.D. thesis, Queen's University, Belfast 1969

Smith, William Allison, *A Historical Study of the Protestant Use of the Bible for Evangelism in India*, Master's thesis, Serampore, India 1966.

Taggart, N.W., *The Irish Factor in World Methodism in the Eighteenth and Nineteenth Centuries*, Ph.D. thesis, Queen's University, Belfast 1981

Index